Learning
to (Re)member
the Things We've Learned
to Forget

Rochelle Brock and Richard Greggory Johnson III
Executive Editors

Vol. 18

The Black Studies and Critical Thinking series
is part of the Peter Lang Education list.
Every volume is peer reviewed and meets
the highest quality standards for content and production.

PETER LANG
New York • Washington, D.C./Baltimore • Bern
Frankfurt • Berlin • Brussels • Vienna • Oxford

Cynthia B. Dillard

Learning *to* (Re)member *the* Things We've Learned *to* Forget

Endarkened Feminisms, Spirituality,
& the Sacred Nature of Research & Teaching

PETER LANG
New York • Washington, D.C./Baltimore • Bern
Frankfurt • Berlin • Brussels • Vienna • Oxford

Library of Congress Cataloging-in-Publication Data
Dillard, Cynthia B.
Learning to (re)member the things we've learned to forget:
endarkened feminisms, spirituality, and the sacred nature of research and teaching /
Cynthia B. Dillard.
p. cm. — (Black studies and critical thinking; vol. 18)
Includes bibliographical references.
1. Womanism. 2. Women, Black. 3. African American women.
4. Blacks—Race identity. I. Title.
HQ1197.D55   305.48'896073—dc23   2011039158
ISBN 978-1-4331-1282-9 (hardcover)
ISBN 978-1-4331-1281-2 (paperback)
ISBN 978-1-4539-0243-1 (e-book)
ISSN 1947-5985

Bibliographic information published by **Die Deutsche Nationalbibliothek**.
Die Deutsche Nationalbibliothek lists this publication in the "Deutsche
Nationalbibliografie"; detailed bibliographic data is available
on the Internet at http://dnb.d-nb.de/.

The paper in this book meets the guidelines for permanence and durability
of the Committee on Production Guidelines for Book Longevity
of the Council of Library Resources.

© 2012 Peter Lang Publishing, Inc., New York
29 Broadway, 18th floor, New York, NY 10006
www.peterlang.com

All rights reserved.
Reprint or reproduction, even partially, in all forms such as microfilm,
xerography, microfiche, microcard, and offset strictly prohibited.

Printed in the United States of America

This book is dedicated to the Mother energy in my life,

To Mother God, for opening a way for this book to come into this world,

To Mother Earth, for your continued abundance and wisdom,

To Grandmother Florence Miller and to my sister, Octavia Lucille Dillard, the mothers who have traveled over the bridge to the other side,

To my Mother Marion Lucille Dillard, who was my way to this world, my model, and my heart,

To my Othermother Wanda Amaker Williams, and my Mother in Ghana, Mrs. Ernestina Ayaw Oppong, both who are love personified,

To my sister mothers Celeste and Judith Dillard,

To those Mothers not named but whose presence has enriched me,

and to the next generation of Mothers,

Taylor Renee Dillard

Henrietta Ayaw Oppong

Morgan K.C. Dillard

May we always (re)member the wisdom of our Mothers.
It is our divine inheritance.

CONTENTS

Preface	ix
Acknowledgments	xiii
CHAPTER ONE	
The Power of Our Cultural Memories: New Visions	1
CHAPTER TWO	
The Seduction of Forgetfulness: (Re)membering Body, Mind, and Spirit	15
CHAPTER THREE	
The Need to Love Blackness: Healing Cultural Memories of African Beauty	29
CHAPTER FOUR	
The Power of Rituals and Traditions:	
(Re)membering African Culture, (Re)membering African Knowledge	41
CHAPTER FIVE	
The Importance of Naming: Spirituality, the Sacred, and New Questions	
for Endarkened Transnational Feminist Research (with Chinwe Okpalaoka)	57
CHAPTER SIX	
Pedagogies of Community Are Pedagogies of the Spirit: Living Ubuntu	83
CHAPTER SEVEN	
The Ability to Create Anew: (Re)membering to Make the World We Want	107
References	117

PREFACE

Memory—of what has been, of acts of commission or omission, of a responsibility abdicated—affects the future conduct of power in any form. (Soyinka, 1999, p. 82)

Colonial and racialized histories have created fragmentation, dislocation, and dismemberment for many African ascendents[1] and other people of color. These entanglements and genealogies of diaspora and location strongly influence the consciousness of African ascendant women throughout the world, even as we negotiate the countless influences that shape and impact both our individual and collective consciousness and particularities as feminists/womanists. These are always and in all ways contested spaces and locations that are deeply spiritual, situated, and embodied. In *Learning to (Re)member the Things We've Learned to Forget: Endarkened Feminisms, Spirituality, and the Sacred Nature of Research and Teaching*, I explore the ways that these histories and spiritualities have shaped Black feminist consciousness and more collective notions of Black womanhood as a cross-cultural diversity of nationalities, socioeconomic classes, sexual identities, spiritual beliefs, and generations.

But what is the center that holds feminism in this diversity *together* for the African ascendant woman, particularly in diaspora? I argue here that a critical part of the answer to this question is found in learning and being *engaged* in our lives and resisting the temptation to compare or create hierarchies of oppression between and among the collective understanding of Black/endarkened feminisms (Lorde, 1970). Such engagements include a deep recognition of the ways that we have been collectively seduced into forgetting who we are as African ascendant women (or have chosen to do so), given the weight and power of our memories and the truly radical act that (re)membering represents in our present lives and work as teachers, as researchers, and as cultural workers. Through the ravages of oppressions such as colonization or slavery and their ever-present inequitable outcomes, we have learned to be both complicit and vigilant in this process of figuring out who we are, who we are becoming. But in order to heal, to put the pieces back together again, we must learn to remember the things that we've learned to forget, including engagements and dialogues in cross-cultural community that theorize our varying spiritualities, experiences, definitions, and meanings of Black womanhood. In this way, (re)membering becomes a

---

1 Given the epistemic nature of language, I use the term "African ascendant" to describe people of African heritage. In contrast to the commonly used term "descendent," Kohain Hahlevi, a Hebrew Israel rabbi uses the term to describe the upward and forward movement of African people on the continent of Africa and in the diaspora. I subscribe to this naming and will use this term throughout this book.

radical and endarkened response to our individual and collective fragmentation at the spiritual and material levels, an endarkened response to the divisions created between mind, body, and spirit, and an endarkened response to our on-going experience and understanding of "what difference difference makes" (Wright, 2003).

Feminist research has both held and contested *experience* as a category of epistemological importance but primarily as a secular one. Absent any attention to spirit, experience is also constructed as absent the sacred. However, the sacred is fundamental to a Black/endarkened feminist epistemology, teaching, and research, given the historical and cultural experiences of African ascendant women worldwide. How can (re)membering bear witness to our individual and collective spiritual consciousness and generate new questions that can inform feminist theory and practice? This book explores that question. Theorizing through sites and journeys across the globe and particularly in Ghana, West Africa, this book explores how spirituality, location, rootedness, experience, and cultural memory engage and create an *endarkened* feminist subjectivity that both (re)members and opens possibilities for research and teaching as sacred practice, as practice that honors the wisdom, history, and cultural productions of African ascendent women particularly and persons of African heritage more generally.

Learning to (Re)member is also a very personal response to Alice Walker's (1983) artistic and political call for Black women to write not only what we want to read but "*all the things [we]* **should** *have been able to read*" (p. 13, emphasis mine). Here, I seek to enact and recognize both the intellectual and creative legacy of African ascendant women as a powerful, provocative, and important "first step" in (re)membering ourselves and in understanding how our knowing and being is rooted in and constantly informed by African wisdom. Even in diaspora, at least part of our ground lies in (re)membering Africa: From my view, this is a critical, sacred, and legitimate space from which the African ascendant can enact teaching and research that also affirms ourselves and our communities. It is also from this exploration that we might embody new visions and models of endarkened feminisms that are truly *trans*national, spiritual, insightful, and creatively *generative*. Ultimately, the work of (re)membering is, as bell hooks (2000) says, all about love...

> So this is a call to love,
> African women scholars and teachers,
> creators of life, of learning.
> Because who we are as (re)searchers
> is best understood by knowing
> what we're struggling *with*,
> (re)searching *for*,

what we're trying to bring into being,
our "projects" in the academy.
But at it's core,
it is all about love.

We are sisters seeking wholeness,
building bridges, and
shaping community
for other courageous scholars.
That means we are sisters making a way for
all
to be who we really are and
to be academic at the same time,
helping us
all
navigate spaces that too often assume we've arrived in the academy
solely because of affirmative action and
not our inherent brilliance,
helping us
all
see that our presence
does not require an extraordinary explanation,
but it does require a whole lot of responsibility and care.
It requires love.

How we love our work and how it blesses us!
We love the drama, the trauma,
the joys and the struggles in our scholarship.
We love it so much that
we are inviting you into the *messy-ness* of it,
into the *regular* parts of our lives,
inviting you to engage in
reciprocal dialogues
that by necessity
question and push,
prod and proclaim and
that always, always, always touch our spirits deeply.
We give homage to those whose work it has been to
sit with us,
talk with us,
feed us,
bandage us up,
hug us,
and remind us of the legacy of African people

who have come before us.
They are the ones who whisper
(and sometimes holler)
"Make a commitment,
tell your truth,
loudly, strongly,
without apology!"
So that's why we do what we do,
that's why we are who we are,
African heritage women,
(re)searching, looking anew for ourselves.
And we are blessed to see her
in the eyes and hearts of each other
and in your eyes too.

Each chapter of *Learning to (Re)member* is based on knowledge and wisdom that we, as African ascendant people generally and African ascendant women particularly, have *learned* to forget. For example, although Chapter 1 suggests that African ascendants have generally forgotten the power of our own memories, Chapter 2 points out that we have also been seduced into forgetting that we are not simply a mind, but body and spirit as African people, too. Chapter 3 takes up the important need to affirm and love Blackness. Chapter 4 and 5 discuss the need to (re)member our rituals and traditions and the importance of naming in African culture, respectively. Chapter 6 suggests that, in these challenging times, we need to (re)member community, a commitment to *Ubuntu* as our lived spirituality. Finally, Chapter 7 reminds us that, from a spiritual and endarkened perspective, we can create the world that we want and need as African people, one that connects the African continent and her diaspora: Spiritual activism and education are the keys to that creation.

And just as we have *learned* to forget, we can also learn to (re)member. This is especially important for those of us whose vocation is teaching and re-search. I have tried, in each of these chapters, to put forth new questions and possibilities for remembering African wisdom within the powerful work of education. I pray that this book might be a step in that direction for us all.

ACKNOWLEDGMENTS

To the Divine Creator of life, who opened the way for this book to come into the world;

To my Henry, the husband and partner whom I am blessed to walk with and lean on in this earthly journey;

To my Family, both given and chosen;

To Dr. Chinwe Okpalaoka, whom I have had the good fortune to write with, learn from, and who has served in so many roles in my life: Co-author, editor, student, confidante, and most importantly as a sisterfriend. May we continue to grow, both as scholar-writers and as African women;

To the other Sisters of the Yam, many who were participants in the first Spirit, Race and Dialogue seminar as well as the *Black Feminist Thought* course in the School of Teaching and Learning at The Ohio State University: Charlotte Bell, Dr. Khosi Kubeka, Dr. Yvette Pierre, Dr. Samatha Wahome and Dr. Ann Waliaula, for their very thoughtful feedback on drafts of Chapter 5, as well as their willingness to help us answer Alice Walker's call to write the texts that we need to read;

To Norman Denzin, for his ever-present mentorship, keen feedback, and the opportunity to debut the first chapter of this book as the Keynote Speech at the 2010 Qualitative Inquiry Congress;

To my fabulous women colleagues, all over the world. While there are simply too many to list, I thank you for your wisdom, conversations, and ever-present glasses of wine;

To Chris Myers, Managing Director at Peter Lang Publishing and to Rochelle Brock, Executive Editor for the Black Studies and Critical Thinking Series at Peter Lang Publishing, for their vision, support, and the important contribution this series makes to (re)membering Black culture;

To The Ohio State University, my former academic institution, which provided the homeplace for much of my academic life including the sabbatical time to reflect, to write and to (re)member this book, and;

To the University of Georgia, my new academic home and a place from which to dream anew.

Photo Acknowledgment

Cover Art: "Sankofa, Our Redemption Song" beaded prayer shawl, created by the author and from the personal collection of Natacha Otey.

Cover photo and photo on page 42: Shellee Fisher Davis, Art of Exposure Photography, shellee@aoephotography.com. All other photos taken by author.

Permissions

Two of the chapters in this book appeared previously in the following publications:

Chapter 1 was the Keynote Address at the 5th Annual Qualitative Inquiry Congress in Urbana-Champaign, Illinois, on May 26, 2010. It is a slightly revised version of Dillard, C. B. (2011). Learning to remember the things we've learned to forget: Endarkened feminisms and the sacred nature of research. In N.K. Denzin & M.D. Giardina (Eds.), *Qualitative inquiry and global crises*. Walnut Creek, CA: Left Coast Press, Inc. The author wishes to gratefully acknowledge Left Coast Press for its permission to use this chapter.

Chapter 5 (co-authored with Chinwe Okpalaoka) is a slightly revised version of Dillard, C.B. & Okpalaoka, C.L. (2011). The sacred and spiritual nature of endarkened transnational feminist praxis in qualitative research. In N. Denzin & Y. Lincoln (Eds.), *The handbook of qualitative research (4th Edition)*. Thousand Oaks, CA: Sage. The co-authors gratefully acknowledge Sage Publications for its permission to use this chapter.

Must be a bond, a connection between us here and us what are across the sea. A connection, the last of the old, first of the new.

—Nana Peazant in "Daughters of the Dust"

Memory is not nostalgia. Memory is specific. One has a relationship to a memory, and it may be a difficult relationship, because a memory always makes a demand on the present.

—Michael Ventura, *A report from El Dorado*

CHAPTER ONE

The Power of Our Cultural Memories

New Visions

Part 1. The question of memory

I can remember the day as if it were yesterday....Ma Vic, with whom I stayed during my time in the village, was not only my dear friend, but my guide in the maze of the market. She had her favorite sellers: The woman from whom she bought baskets of plump red tomatoes, another woman, her plantain, another, yam, still another, her spices and food staples. And as a regular customer, her loyalty was rewarded with the expected "dash" of a few extra onions or an additional handful of rice. As Vic very confidently maneuvered her way through the market, I warily negotiated the open sewers, the sharp corners of the metal roofs, and the young market women who, without a stall, carried their store—big trays of fish or mango or other goods—on their heads. So, my eyes faced downward most of the time, tenuously watching every step. My observations of the market were primarily at the places where we stopped to make a purchase, the places where my eyes could focus on what was around me and not on my feet.

We stopped at the plantain woman's stall. "My sister!" the woman exclaimed, greeting Vic with the enthusiasm of someone who knows she's going to make a big sale. "You are welcome," she said to me, the customary greeting in Ghana when you haven't seen someone for a while. Her smile was warm, seeming to (re)member my presence on previous visits to her stall. Exchanging more small talk in Twi, Vic and the woman began their search for the biggest and the best plantains in the pile. And that's when our eyes met. About 70 years old, this woman (possibly the aunt or mother of the seller) was sitting in the shadows of the stall. She stared at me, a clear combination of curiosity and suspicion in her eyes, which were yellowed with age. She looked me up and down. I smiled at her, very uncomfortable with her unwavering gaze. As Vic and the seller were finishing their transaction, the old woman reached over and touched Vic's arm, her face now absolutely perplexed, nodding in my direction: "What **is** she (me)? Is she a White woman?" I nearly fell over, a rush of emotions running through me, from absolute horror to disgust to disbelief to sadness. Vic giggled and explained to the woman (who had still not quit staring at me) that I was not a White woman but a Black American. But that evening in my researcher's journal (and through confused, angry and sad tears that could've filled a river), I wondered aloud as I wrote: "How could she see *me* as a White woman?" "Couldn't she see the African woman I could see in myself?" "Didn't she know what had happened to millions of Africans who'd been forcibly taken from the shores of Ghana and other West African countries?" "Where did she think we had gone?" "Had she never imagined that some of us would return?" "How can this sister/mother see me this way?" In reflection, what frightened me most about her question was that, at that very moment, I couldn't answer it myself:

> What had been the rather solid taken-for-granted nature of my African American identity—an identity that I'd used to make sense of myself—melted down like butter on a hot summer's day in that moment in Ghana. Something very rich that I loved dearly had become useless fat on the sidewalk, no help whatsoever in explaining and understanding what she saw, or who I was. But I know there is wisdom in her question or it wouldn't have come to teach me a lesson. If I'm to "be" a researcher in this space, I will have to struggle with the butter on the sidewalk, the shifting ground of African identity through Ghanaian eyes. Neither here nor there (Ghana or the U.S.), neither African nor American, neither recognizably Black nor White. Maybe it's not either/or: Maybe it's both/and? Somehow, it feels like it's beyond these dualities. They seem too simple. Regardless, it hurts to do this work. (Journal, 1/22/98).

And this pain stayed with me until the following week, when market day came again:

> Today is market day again. Honestly, I'm dreading it. But I don't think there's an acceptable excuse not to go and help....As we approached the plantain seller's stall, my stomach churned and my nerves were shattered, afraid of what "insult" (however innocent) would come from the old lady. Vic, oblivious to my inner turmoil, again greeted the plantain woman and went about her business. But before I could properly greet the seller, I glanced to my right and caught the eye—and the smile—of the old lady. "Morning, Black American lady! How are you?" she says happily, clearly concentrating hard to speak to me in her heavily accented English. I replied in my equally faltering Twi: "Me ho ye." ("I'm fine.") And she reached over and grabbed my wrist. "Black American. Yea." (Journal, 1/29/98)

This story is from my 2006 book *On Spiritual Strivings: Transforming an African American Woman's Academic Life*. In the book, I sought to examine the ways that centering spirituality in an academic life transforms its very foundations, creating the site for spiritual healing and service to the world. And I chose to begin this chapter with this particular story because it is still on my mind and in my heart, gnawing in the pit of my gut. *"What is she? Is she a White woman? A Black American—yea!"* Both the question and the way the old lady asked it threw my entire sense of who I was into confusion. Yet, in retrospect, it is in the answer to that question that I have come to better understand my self, my life's purpose and a new direction for the work as a teacher and researcher. Here, I want to try to reflexively read and (re)member this story and so many others created and lived by Black women everywhere, to make visible the spiritual and cultural nature of (re)membering that is necessary to truly appreciate the complex and contested spaces and places of Black women's lives in our fullness. What I am also suggesting here is that, you the reader (not unlike my teacher education students in the university) must travel with me on this journey, in the same engaged process of (re)membering and seeing what Busia (1989) calls our cultural artifacts or "icons of significance" (p. 201) as well. This is our (re)search and teaching together, in community, the goal being to develop a better sense truly being able to *see* Africa's people at home and in the diaspora. And while my memory of the market in Ghana may seem like a very private and singular story of travel, journey, awakening, and cultural memory, it might also be read and considered as representative of the collective history of African peoples as we traverse and settle, move, and create homeplace, wherever we are on the globe. These memories are about the concrete aspects of our lives, where meaning—within our memories—"becomes what we can read and what we can no longer or could never read about ourselves and our lives" (Busia, 1989, p. 198). Busia goes on to say that

> This act of reading becomes an exercise in *identifications* to recognize life experiences and historic transformations that point the way toward a celebration, a coming together attainable only through an understanding and acceptance of the demands of the past, which are transformed into a gift of the future. (p. 198, emphasis mine)

In essence, we will read and hear differently and at varying depths depending on our ability to read *productively*, to read the signs along the way.

Central to my thinking about the meanings of culture and race in education and other decolonizing projects is an often unnamed element of identity, one that is inherent in the acts of research and teaching, and deeply embedded in the act of memory and of (re)membering. Often in research by scholars of color and others, we see that racial and/or cultural memory is at least part of what is raised up in our on-going quest to be seen, heard and unlimited in the diverse ways we approach our questions, our scholarship (see Alexander, 2005; Coloma, 2008; Daza, 2008; Strong-Wilson, 2008; Subedi, 2008; Subreendeth, 2008, for examples). In common, memory can be thought of as a thing, person, event that brings to mind and heart a past experience and with it, not only the ability to (re)member (to recall and think of *again*), but to also put back together. The *American Heritage Dictionary* (2000) goes so far as to say that to (re)member is "to bear in mind, as deserving a gift or reward" (p. 597). And the very intimate nature of research narratives like the story from Ghana that began this chapter suggests that memory is also about an awakening, an opening to the spirit of something that has, until that moment, been asleep within us.

For many researchers of color, embracing an ethic that opens to spirit is fundamental to the nature of learning, teaching, and by extension, research. We recognize that such spaces and acts—and our memories and ways of being with/in them—are always and in all ways also political, cultural, situated, embodied, and spiritual: They are alive and present within us. However, all too often, we have been seduced into forgetting (or have chosen to do so), given the weight and power of our memories and the often radical act of (re)membering in our present lives and work, that is (re)membering as an act of decolonization. And if we assume as I do that the knowledge, wisdom, and ways of our ancestors are a central and present part of everything that has existed, is existing, and will exist in what we call the future, then teaching and research must also undertake an often unnamed, unrecognized, unarticulated and forgotten task that is important for individuals who yearn to understand ways of being and knowing that have been marginalized in the world and in formal education. Simply put, *we must learn to (re)member the things that we've learned to forget*. Whether wandering into unfamiliar or always familiar contexts, making conscious choices to use or not use languages and cultural wisdom, or strategically choosing to cover or uncover (Yoshino, 2006), in leaning on cultural memory and in the acts of (re)membering, an awakening in research and teaching is possible and powerful. And there are several lessons we must learn in order to (re)member, in order to answer the question asked by the old lady: "What is she?"—and by extension, what are *we*? The first lesson we must recognize and (re)member is embedded in that very story, a lesson that many African ascendant people already know:

That being scattered in diaspora is an act of dispossession from our past, from connections to our culture, original homelands, languages and from each other. We must (re)member in order to be whole.

According to Busia (1989) (re)membering is being able "to see again the fragments that make up the whole, not as isolated individual and even redundant fragments, but as part of a creative and sustaining whole" (p. 197). So at least part of the old lady's questions is about (re)membering as an act of piece-gathering, of collecting and assembling fragments of a larger whole, of creating and innovating identity for African people that includes African Americans. But the bigger part of this lesson, particularly important for teacher education and research preparation, is about seeing ourselves in the gaze of another and not looking away, but instead looking deeper. It is fundamentally about answering the question: Who are we in *relation* to one another? —and staying long enough to find out.

THE POWER OF OUR CULTURAL MEMORIES

Part II: A memory in time: Praisesong for the Queen Mother[1]

You woke me this morning,
and I became part of Your divine plan,
chosen on this day
to be among the living.
You dressed me in a purple kaba[2]
and I became the color of royalty,
traveling to the village in a dirty old van
that felt like my royal carriage,
the curtains drawn for the privacy
of the new Queen Mother.
You introduced "Professor Cynthia Dillard"
to the Chiefs of the kingdom,
and I became my own desire
to know as I am known.
You honored my family name
on the front of the community center and preschool,
and I became my parents, their parents, parents, parents,
those who, by virtue of the Blackness of Africa,
were considered by some
not to be fully human,
but whose depth of humanity shone like the sun in this moment.
You brought my sister-mothers to bathe me in the soothing waters of life,
and I once again became the child of all my mothers,
Marion Lucille Cook Dillard
Wanda Amaker Williams
Florence Mary Miller
Nana Mansa, the first
and those mothers whose names I do not know.
You wrapped me in cloth of traditional kente,
and I became the weavers of that cloth,
the men who learned from their fathers and their fathers' fathers,
an art so special that it had taken months and months
of skill, patience, and love in its creation.
You sat me on my Queen's stool

---

1   Becoming a Queen Mother is part of a collection of meditations from an unpublished manuscript entitled *Living Africa: A Book of Meditations*. This is also in honor of Paule Marshall's *Praisesong for the Widow (1983)*, a book that has had a profound influence on my thoughts on the endarkened nature of memory.

2   Kaba is a style of dress worn by Ghanaian women, made from Batik/wax print cloth. It consists of a fitted top, often embellished with very elaborate necklines, sleeves and waist and a form-fitting skirt with a slit and a head wrap.

and I became Nana Mansa II, Nkosua Ohemaa[3]
the spirit of Nana Mansa the first now residing
not in my head,
but in the stool.
She speaks centuries of cultural memories
directly to my African American heart,
"I had many children, but you are the only one who has returned."
You lovingly dress me in beads old and new,
adorning my fingers with gold rings, my Queen's chain around my neck,
and I became the precious riches and treasures of the Universe
both now and then.
You fanned me with cloth and palms branches and bare hands,
and I became the wind,
carrying Your voice:
> "Don't be afraid, Nana.
> Trust me.
> You have all that you need.
> I will show you what you already know."

You poured libation,
and called me into the sacred ritual of (re)membering,
and I became my own full circle as a researcher,
a searcher again, honoring the knowledge of
who and what is here and there,
of what's been and is to be.
Inseparable realities, united by Your gift of breath
a committed teacher and student of my own becoming.
You drummed and we danced,
and with each beat,
I became the rhythms of my passed on ancestors
who gathered with us on that day
along with brothers and sisters of the village, the community, the diaspora,
a holy encounter indeed!
You gave food to feed those gathered,
and I became my own full belly
and the too often empty bellies
of the village children and families.
But for that moment, we were all satisfied,

---

3   Nkosua Ohemaa, in the Twi language means Queen Mother of Development. Persons are chosen for this role by the Chief and Elders of the Village and have the responsibility for developing the Village. Such roles typically include leadership in social and economic development projects such as bringing electricity or water sources to the village, building and maintaining schools and clinics, etc. While the stool of the Queen Mother of Development is not required to be given through matrilineal or clan affiliation, a woman selected for this role serves alongside with the Chief of the Village for life.

full,
happy,
joyful in Your bounty.
You've blessed me with life,
a chance to manifest extraordinary works
through You, Great Creator.
By becoming all of myself,
I can live not into the smallness of the world's expectations,
but into the greatness of the true names,
You've given to me.

Praisesongs are traditional types of poems, sung in various locations all over the continent of Africa. They are ceremonial and social poems, recited or sung at public celebrations such as outdoorings,[4] anniversaries or funerals. Embracing the history, legends and traditions of a community of people, praisesongs can be used to celebrate or affirm triumph over adversity, bravery and courage both in life and death. They can also mark social transition and upward movement culturally, socially, or spiritually. While the meditation above is a praisesong to my ascent as a Queen Mother in Ghana, here's the pertinent question for those who teach and research: *How might our memories, our encounters, and the representations of our memories act as praisesongs in the world?* As we teach, conduct research, and examine and create "texts" (whether the research narrative, the lesson plan, the interview transcript, the representational text in publication), our sense of who we are, our identity, our very selves and spirits are seen, understood, recognized, and grounded in our past: They make sense to us based on something that has happened (in memory) versus simply as a present moment or a future not yet come. I am arguing here that it is from our memories that we can recognize and better answer the question: "Who am I?" and collectively "Who are we?" This isn't just about being able to recognize times past on a calendar or datebook. This is fundamentally to see that our known, unknown, and yet-to-be-known lives as human being are deeply imbued with meaning that is based in our memories. Booth (2006) suggests that in order to answer the question of who we are, we have to go deep into the well of memory

> to draw a boundary between group members and others; to provide a basis for collective action; and to call attention to life-in-common, a shared history and future....All of these involve claims about identity across time and change, and about identity and responsibility as well....Statement[s] of identity turn out to involve a strong *temporal* dimension. (p. 3, emphasis mine)

---

4   An outdooring is a traditional ceremony in which the birth of a new baby is celebrated, named and brought "outdoors" for all to admire and welcome into the community.

This is also fundamental to an African cosmology, one that is based on understanding one's place, space, and purpose in time through recognition of a common or communal destiny: *I am because we are*. And for those of us who think and feel ourselves into our scholarship through frameworks and paradigms that embrace African knowledges and sensibilities and that "just *feel* right to us" (Lorde, 1984), we also recognize that we cannot feel or engage our scholarship without seeing that, Dianne Reeves (1999) suggests in her song "Testify":

> God and time are synonymous/and in time God reveals all things/
> Be still/
> Stand in love/
> and pay attention.

Within African spaces, time is not thought of in the abstract, but in relation to Spirit. Time is what has happened here, what continues to happen here, and the honoring of "the relationships that linger [here]" (Bargna, 2000, p. 25). This is one of the major ways that African cosmology challenges Western conceptions of time, space, and location: It is circular, based in past, present, and future as intricate connective and collective webs of meaning making:

> You honored my family name
> on the front of the community center and preschool,
> And I became my parents, their parents, parents, parents,
> Those who, by virtue of the Blackness of Africa
> Were considered by some
> Not to be fully human...

So that brings us to the second lesson:

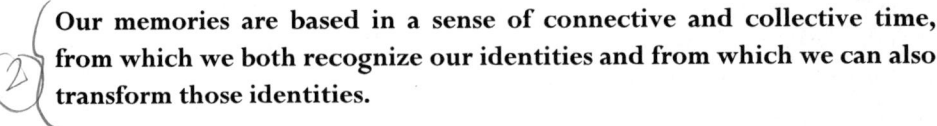

Our memories are based in a sense of connective and collective time, from which we both recognize our identities and from which we can also transform those identities.

And where do we see Africa in the memory of African people in the diaspora? For example, research of the African American rarely explicitly acknowledges the importance of the transatlantic slave trade and the Middle Passage as relevant in the collective memory of African ascendant personhood. The Middle Passage was the forced enslavement and forced journey of millions of Africans from the continent of Africa to the New World. Spaces associated with this trade in human beings—the slave dungeons that dot the Western coast of countries like Ghana and Senegal, the routes and rivers that were used for the inland walk to those coastal forts and dungeons, sites in the U.S. that commemorate the places where enslaved African people resisted and created new homes, new communities—these sites are ripe with memory and with meaning for African ascendent peoples who *chose* to (re)member, who *choose* to make pilgrimage to these spaces to feel, see, and better understand the place of such memories in the formations of our identities, our personhood (Dillard & Bell, 2011; Dillard, 2008). And while the events of the Middle Passage and slavery in the New World are now centuries old (and often unrecognized in the memories of many, both on the continent of Africa and in the diaspora), for those who choose to (re)member, these engagements have the profound ability to transform us, to bring us back to places (both literally and spiritually) that we heard in the praisesong: *"I had many children, but you were the one who returned."* How do we see these recognitions in our scholarship? Busia (1989) says this: "*Everything* about the placing of the questions of research is important here, as our lives and those of the participants we study are full of 'icons of significance'" (p. 201, emphasis mine). With every question we ask or don't ask, answer or don't answer, it is crucial for us to recognize and see that our students and research participants are being forced to ask central questions of their lives as well. As we are studying literacy practices, or examining teacher education, or looking at the ways that African American culture shapes mathematics instruction, what does it really mean to ask: "*Tell me about yourself*." Where is the place of cultural memory of the Middle Passage in that question, both for the researched and the researcher? This is key, as so many of us "study" with/in/about African ascendant communities, often without the requisite sense of cultural memory needed to meaningfully read and understand what we are seeing. How do we (or might we) recognize the child we are observing as an *African* American, as connected to and collectively a part of the circle of African time? How is our entire system of education shaped by the lack of our own memories (or knowledge) of an event like the Middle Passage, one so very traumatic that it forever changed the very time, space, and spirit of humanity in that there would have been no African diaspora, no African Americans without it?

Irwin-Zarecka (1994) states: "Personal relevance of the traumatic memory and not personal witness to the trauma [is what] defines community" (p. 49). But the power and relevance of the memory *endures*. It matters. An African cosmology requires that we see and better understand this persistence across time (its enduringness as described by Booth, 2006), as its presence describes one of the ways that the African community is bounded, has borders and cultural understandings that bind and define its members. Such boundedness within community when conscious and connected transforms one's identity such that the question "Who am I?" is no longer a total and bewildering mystery for African Americans and others in diaspora. It may become, as we saw in the earlier praisesong, imbued with meaning and with response-ability, both of which are at the core of claims to membership from an endarkened feminist epistemology (see Dillard, 2000, 2006a; Dillard & Okpalaoka, 2011). It is the space where we find our identities are much more expansive than what we may have believed.

One of the many ways that African feminist scholars working within endarkened frameworks are (re)membering or putting back together notions of time that honor and lift up "the relationships that linger there," is to attempt to ask a different set of questions, starting first with ourselves. These are the echoes that were heard in the praisesong, an interrogation of the ways that memory is always already there. It is the way that the sacred also shapes memory and is inseparable in memory. Within the temporal and physical movement that Africans in diaspora have undergone, it is also what gives the memory shape within Western epistemological frameworks, including within the frameworks of feminism (Dillard & Okpalaoka, 2011). It is embedded in the ways that a researcher can (re)member, can put herself back together again:

> By becoming all of myself,
> I can live not into the smallness of the world's expectations,
> but into the greatness of the true names
> You've given to me.

What is needed are models of inquiry that truly honor the complexities of memories. Of indigenous and "modern" time, experienced not just in our minds, but in our bodies and spirits as well. Frameworks that approach teaching and research as sacred practices, worthy of reverence. Ways of thinking, feeling and engaging teaching and research that honors the fluidity of time and space, of the material world and the spiritual one. Mostly, as we point out in recent work located in the slave dungeons in Ghana (Dillard & Bell, 2011), we need a way to inquire that acknowledges both the joy and pain of history and contemporary times, of location and dislocation and the transformation of both in our work. African women's voices and experiences, regardless where we find ourselves on the globe tend not to be stories of a singular self, but stories of *we*, collective stories deeply embedded in African women's indigenous knowledges. And these stories are also imbued with wisdom. In his discussion of the Middle Passage, Tom Feelings (1995) eloquently states:

> I began to see how important the telling of this particular story could be for Africans all over the world, many who consciously or unconsciously share this race memory, this painful experience of the Middle Passage....But if this part of history could be told in such a way that those chains of the past...could, in the telling, become spiritual links that willingly bind us together now and into the future, then that painful Middle Passage could become, ironically, a positive connecting line to all of us, whether living inside or outside the continent of Africa. (p. ii)

Formed as a question, what do such memories mean for the teacher/scholar of color (and those embodying a critical consciousness) and how might we more explicitly and systematically engage them, (re)member what we have forgotten as a way toward healing not just ourselves but those with whom we teach and do research? Turning back to Feelings (1995) above, he suggests first that such memories, from a spiritual framework, have the potential to connect those on the continent of Africa to those in the diaspora, the result of the traumatic acts of the trans-Atlantic slave trade. This is a central and defining characteristic of cultural memories for all who live with/in diaspora: *These are memories that acknowledge an ever present thread between the diaspora and the continent, a heritage "homeplace."* It is not accidental that many scholars of color take up the exploration and research into/about connections to or with/in some version of an ancestral, heritage, or cultural homeplace and that our representations—in art, in inquiry, in personhood and identity—represent those cultural spaces and places. Secondly, *cultural memories are intimate*: They are memories that, good or bad, make you ache with desire "to find the marriage of meaning and matter in our lives, in the world" (Mountain Dreamer, 2005, p. 42). I believe this may be true for Whites and others who have not carried or been politically or culturally marked or "racialized" and is worthy of being explored by all researchers, regardless of race (Mazzei, 2007). Such intimacy is inextricably linked to racial and cultural identities, that is, memories are part and parcel of the meanings of identity, of the meaning of who we are and how we are in the world. Husband (2007), in his work on African American male teacher identity, suggests that cultural memories are those memories of experiences and/or events related to collective and or individual cultural identity "that are either too significant to easily forget or so salient that one strives to forget" (p. 10). He goes on to describe the fundamental nature and character of cultural memories:

> In the case of the former, racial/cultural memories can be thought of as memories of events as cultural beings that are/were so remarkable that we consider them to be defining moments in our life histories....Pertaining to the latter, race/cultural memories are those related to our cultural identities that are so potent [often painful] that we tend to suppress [them] in order to function as human beings. (p. 10)

What we see here is that the intimate nature of cultural memories and their work in identity creation is inseparable from what it means to be vulnerable in our work as educators and researchers. It requires a reaching down inside of one's self and across towards others to a place that may "break your heart" (Behar, 1996) but, like many courageous teacher and researchers, *choosing to go there anyhow.*

That brings us to the final part of a definition of cultural memories: *They are memories that change our ways of being (culture) and knowing (epistemology) in what we call* the present. They are inspirational, breathing new life into the work of teaching, research, and living. They are the roots we must first grow in order to have leaves. They are memories that transform us, a place within and without that feeds our ability to engage new metaphors and practices in our work (Dillard, 2000).

Part 3: The claim of memory

Here's lesson #3:

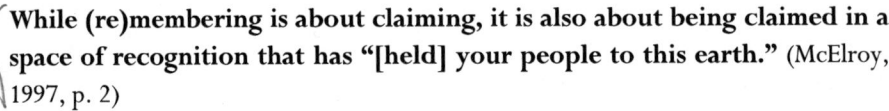

While (re)membering is about claiming, it is also about being claimed in a space of recognition that has "[held] your people to this earth." (McElroy, 1997, p. 2)

> *It's been lights off (no electricity) since about 7 pm. Around 7:30 pm, the seamstress arrives with my dresses. They are both really beautiful. But so was what happened with the purple kaba (skirt and top). The seamstress asked me to go and try it on so she could make any adjustments that might be needed. Given my experience with the old lady in the market, I was a little leery about what she might say once I put the dress on. I carefully tied my head wrap and tentatively came out of the side room. "Hmmmmm," she exclaimed, looking at me in my kaba, clearly in admiration. "Who tied it for you?" she said, pointing to my head wrap. "I did it," I said, realizing that I had done so in a manner that surprised her. "Turn around," she said sternly. And as her hand brushed down the back side of my body, I knew that, like the looks of admiration from a group of brothers earlier in the day, she too recognized [another] one of the many carry-overs of African womanhood that could not be oppressed or suppressed, even through the violence of the slave trade: The African woman's backside in a slit skirt. She turned to Vic: "She is an African woman." So, however weak were our identifications of these links between us, as African women, they were clear and apparent to her and to me in that moment. And her look of recognition is one I will never, ever forget. (Journal, 1/22/98)*

Irwin-Zarecka (1994) speaks brilliantly of how people make sense of the past, particularly relevant to this discussion of memories and personhood of African people. That is that, in a wholly racialized society, our collective memories are less about an intellectual "truth" than they are about what we are referencing, what we are working to construct, what we desire to put back together again. Mostly, these memories bear weight on the experiences being (re)membered for these different groups and shape claims to "mine," "theirs," "ours." That is what makes them cultural memories. I am arguing here that such memory work is critical for marginalized peoples, in order to see ourselves more clearly, in order to see how we are mutually recognized, mutually (re)membered, mutually mediated (Anzaldúa, 1999; Moraga & Anzaldúa, 1981; Fernandes, 2003). They are the memories that reference the place that holds us to this earth, the ways we are because we have been. However, (re)membering in this way is not sufficient if revisioning education for African ascendant people is the goal. From an endarkened feminist stance, engaging cultural memories must move through and beyond the dualities that identity formation too often constructs, the binary and exclusionary identities based in opposition and in the "too-other" (Collins, 2000, p. 70). It is important for the reader to be clear here: I am not suggesting that the identity categories of race, class, gender, sexuality, nation-state, etc., be ignored. Rather, I am suggesting that engaging cultural memories, in all their diversity, is a way toward also (re)membering our *spiritual* identities. Drawing on African women's ways of knowing both culturally and spiritually might provide a space to explore more fully our diversity as African women on the continent and in diaspora. This is explicitly what my sister co-author and I take up in Chapter 5, advocating a more sacred practice of research and teaching. However, from an endarkened feminist framework, exploring the power of spiritual identity and spirituality is a way to engage an interconnectedness with those with whom we work, teach and research, seeking a deeper common ground that such relationships might bring as an essential part of the endeavor. The goal? To see the work of defining and developing consciousness of Black womanhood through cultural memories as the work of both the teacher and the taught, the researcher and the researched, recognizing always that while the process may make more clear our collective identity as Black women, it is still subjective and always partial. However, according to Irwin-Zarecka (1994),

> it is the definition shared by people we study that matters. In many cases there is a rather radical difference between the observer's and the participant's realities....But whether the past as we understand it and the past as understood by our subjects are closer or further apart, we ought to consider both in our analysis. Our baseline is a needed standard for critical judgment and their baseline is what informs remembrance [and hence, the answers]. (p. 19)

In many ways, Irwin-Zarecka positions the teacher and researcher as a narrator and creator of memory, both her/his own and the collective memory of the hearts and soul of humanity, in all its variations. However, for the Black or endarkened feminist teacher/researcher whose work is often deliberately situated in indigenous spaces and places and focused on (re)membering knowledge and its consequent cultural production, this is not simply the narration of memory: It is the *deliberate* work of engaging and *preserving* these memories, both the memory itself and our engagements and experiences with it. But, it is also our *duty*—our responsibility—to *(re)member*: We are those who can bear witness to our African "past," diasporic "present," and "future" as a full circle. That is after all what it means to be in community, to be in the spirit collectively.

CHAPTER TWO

The Seduction of Forgetfulness

(Re)membering Body, Mind, and Spirit

> All writing is confession. Confession masked and revealed in the voices and faces of our characters. All is hunger. The longing to be known fully and still loved. The admission of our own inherent vulnerability, our weakness, our tenderness of skin, fragility of heart, our overwhelming desire to be relieved of the burden of ourselves in the body of another, to be forgiven of our ultimate aloneness in the mystical body of a god or the common work of revolution. These are human considerations that the best of [teachers, researchers] presses her fingers upon. (Moraga, 1993)

Seduce: 1) to entice someone astray from right behavior; 2) to lead away from duty, accepted principles or proper conduct.

Forget: 1) to be unable to (re)member something; 2) to treat with thoughtless inattention, neglect; 3) to leave behind unintentionally; 4) to fail to mention.

Seduction is, seduction ain't...

Learning to (re)member is about recognizing and examining our seductions: Those irresistible moments when we have been enticed away from ourselves, led away from our duties, and have accepted others' principles or notions of identity and proper conduct as our own. Typically, we think of seductions as dangerous, mostly sexual, lurid, and with certain implications of the body. In our imaginary, seductions are primarily secret, private, and intimate affairs, maybe not appropriate trysts or spaces of analysis for "proper" academics. In Judith Butler's *Bodies That Matter* (1993) she asserts that all bodies are involved in a culturally and politically mediated process whereby certain bodies are designated as important (that is, they *matter*) and others as unimportant, unworthy of recognition and certainly of respect. Many have spoken of the all too often tortuous history of Black women's bodies, of our being characterized as non-being, virtual blank slates, and the ultimate Other for inscription of White male dominance, sites of hatred and abuse (Bethel, 1982; Christian, 1985; hooks, 1989; Madison, 2009; Moraga & Anzaldúa, 1981; Rogers, 2000). This history of seductions and of forgettings, both intentional and as a means of survival for African ascendant people is well documented (Hilliard, 1995; Husband, 2007; King, 2005; Smith, 1983).

Taking my cue from Soyini Madison (2009) and her provocative idea of flipping the script on the notion of danger in ethnography, I would like here to put the notion of seduction under scrutiny, to reposition seduction of/from individuals and communities so that it can be seen "to now include the structures of power that generate and sustain what is dangerous (in this case, seductive) to *all* of us..." (p. 189, emphasis hers). Here, I pose specific questions to African ascendant people: What are the seductions, particularly related to education, that have had detrimental effects on our minds, bodies, and spirits? How do we (re)member as a way of talking back to the power of these seductions, resisting them, and recognizing our own power in the process?

According to Irwin-Zarecka (1994) taking up seduction within the context of our cultural memories suggests a need to examine how the past is made to matter "by whom, to whom, when, where and why...[as] different people care about their pasts in different ways" (pp. 8–9). For African ascendant people, gathering and working through the fragmented mosaic of our collective cultural memories across the diaspora and in/on the continent of Africa suggests a deep engagement with *what* has seduced us collectively such that we can more clearly recognize *how* these seductions have been marshaled for and against us, how we have been complicit in that seduction, and what we might do now to resist seductions that do not serve our humanity. One possibility for such resistance is through using a differing set of theories, based in cultural memories, to guide us in examining our work "from the tip to the root, from the surface to the foundation" (Madison, 2009, p. 190). Through this process, we might cast into relief not only *how* we've been seduced into forgetting historically but *what* we might choose to (re)member and what we want those (re)memberings to do.

It is important to note that I am not speaking here of the on-going and historical distinctions in the literature that have been made between memory and history. Halbwach's (1926 [1950]) early work on the social nature of memory as a tool for how one develops a sense of belonging to a particular group provided a site from which a number of scholars have developed a substantial body of work on collective memory and identity (Rodriguez & Fortier, 2007; Booth, 2006; Rogers, 2000). These scholars and thinkers further suggest how, as memory disappears or is forgotten, sites of memory become the spaces for collective (re)membering and sites of construction through which political consciousness and movements towards social justice happen. And, colonial and racialized histories—and the seductions related to them—have created fragmentation, dislocation, and dismemberment for many African ascendants and other people of color from their cultural and spiritual foundations. However, Black and endarkened feminist scholars have brilliantly illuminated the place of cultural memories in addressing these ruptures and their particular relevance for women of African heritage across the globe (Alexander, 2005; Brand, 2001; Busia, 1993, 1989; hooks, 2008, 1993; Marshall, 1984; Wekker, 1997). These entanglements and genealogies of diaspora and location strongly influence the consciousness of African ascendant people, especially as we negotiate the countless seductions that have shaped and impacted both our individual and collective consciousness. While I speak here of how acts of (re)membering might provide spaces of resistance to political, cultural, and social seductions for African ascendant people, I am also arguing that (re)membering as a response will always and in all ways also raise up contested cultural spaces and locations that are deeply spiritual, situated, and embodied (Alexander, 2005; Anzaldúa, 1999; Dillard, 2009; hooks, 1993). Thus, (re)membering becomes a radical response to our individual and collective fragmentation at the cultural, spiritual, *and* material levels, a response to the false divisions created between mind, body, and spirit. It is also a response to our on-going experiences and understanding of difference and identity, the sticky, sometimes uncharted, spaces both within a collective African heritage and across our multiple identity differences.

The task of bringing cultural memory to bear is not necessarily easy work, as seduction creates powerful sites of amnesia, often masked as nostalgia, colorblindness, or "universal" theories and cultural production that have created very strong frames in the individual and collective cultural memories of systems of education, of societies and nations of the world. But as Soyinka (1999) reminds us, for African ascendants, the process of (re)membering is also about articulating one's sense of belonging, of place, a certain sort of Truth telling, where

> the very process of its exposition becomes part of the necessity and, depending on the nature of the past that it addresses, the impact it has made on the lives of her citizens and the toll it has taken on their sense of belonging, it may be regarded as being capable of guaranteeing or foundering the future of a nation. (p. 12)

However difficult, defining ourselves for ourselves is necessary work for all human beings, regardless of nation. It is fundamentally at the heart of what it means to be educated. And coming to terms with and consciousness of complex and often troubling memories and legacies as African ascendant people in relation with/to diverse others and ourselves will require us to chose from and fill in the blanks of often disparate and sometimes competing cultural memories. However, the outcome might yield the development of a greater sense of responsibility to being full human beings, as African people, with appreciation for the spirituality and diversity of our memories and stories. It may also be seen as a response to and even revisioning of Du Bois'

(1903/1989) still-relevant notion of double consciousness, creating a broader vision in which our consciousness as Black people includes analysis of how our minds, bodies, *and* spirits situate us as individuals *within* a collective and are known to us *through* the collective. The power of Du Bois' notion of Black consciousness brings a particular responsibility for African ascendant researchers and teachers. We see a brilliant example of this in Denzel Washington's portrayal of Melvin Tolson in the film *The Great Debaters*. In a very poignant scene, an African American student disrespects Tolson's role as an African American teacher and disregards (or chooses not to (re)member) the long legacy of struggle for formal education experienced by African American people in the United States. Denzel Washington's stinging response to the student is this: "I, like every other professor at this school, am here to help you find, take back and keep your righteous mind because, obviously, you have lost it" (Weinstein & Washington, 2007). While the responsibility of African ascendant people and teaching will be discussed in more detail in Chapter 6, the task in deconstructing the myriad of seductions within systems of education should be seen as no less than a "taking back" of our righteous minds, bodies, and spirits.

The danger of seduction, the "danger" of the spiritual

I was invited to present a paper at a conference on art, culture, and politics at the University of Cape Coast in 2003. About 200 people attended, most from Ghana but also from Nigeria, Ivory Coast, Kenya, Togo, and the United States. I noticed right away the handful of women of African heritage at the conference. I was the only African American woman in attendance, the remaining participants from the United States being European American males from various higher education institutions. As consecutive panels gathered on the podium and presented their conference papers, I became more disconcerted, recognizing the deeply entrenched and global nature of the meaning of being a "researcher," as one who engages in "research" that is primarily quantitative and largely cognitive/psychological study. Although those in attendance represented diverse countries and were predominately of African heritage, it was clear that we'd *all* been trained in Western theories and notions of research, with little resistance or critical examination of how such training had shaped our pedagogies and approaches to research. We'd literally been trained away from ourselves. Part of what that meant for me was also the rather blatant absence of any talk of spirituality. The spiritual nature of research, the spiritual outcomes of research, and the influences of the researcher as a spiritual being were unmentioned and unnamed in project after project. To be an African researcher, for this collection of scholars, was to embrace a doctrine of detachment and separation, to be a part of the worldwide Enlightenment project as Marimba Ani (1994) so clearly articulated years ago. And we'd learned our lessons well. I said a silent prayer and shared my paper, one that was in direct contradiction and resistance to these lessons, an examination of the spiritual nature of African-centered and feminist research! At the break, a brother-scholar boldly (and rather brashly) approached me, definitely more eager to make a point than to ask a question. The accusation in his tone was clear: "Professor Dillard, if every interaction and everything I do is spiritual, then how do we measure one piece of research against another? How will we know if our research is 'good'?"

Watch out: Theory and the material world

Within a capitalistic society, seductions are powerful, pervasive, and real. They exert pressure and force at every turn. Recognizing the myriad of seductions that encourage forgetfulness, I would like to examine two primary seductions in education embodied in the previous memory, raising some of the deleterious effects of these seductions for African ascendant people.

The seduction and rewards of "theory"

A primary seduction that has great relevance in research and teaching and that is particularly dangerous to African ascendant people is the seduction of science, the seduction of theory as "Truth" as that which is definable, observable, and explainable (Lather, 2007). Its paradox is embodied in the question posed to me by the African brother-scholar: "How will we know what *good* research is?" The question always already assumes that something called "good" research exists, is conducted in a particular way, and most importantly, is found desirable by everyone. There's also the assumption that whatever good research and theorizing is, it is something done solely by an elite group who call ourselves researchers or scholars (Lemert, 2010). Like Lemert, I am arguing against this seduction, putting forth the notion that "most people whatever their social class, age, gender, race, or sexual orientation develop a good enough repertoire of social theories" (p. 1). Everyone theorizes. It's how human beings make sense of our lives and work. Some of us just theorize as our vocation. But the seduction of theory also refers to the ways that research texts considered scholarly (read "good," legitimate, or worthy) are also held in high esteem or privileged by a predominately patriarchal, racist, xenophobic, often classist and homophobic hegemony (Dillard & Dixson, 2006; Trinh, 1989). So to interrogate the scholar's comment (as well as reflexively examine the doubt that I personally held about my own work in that conference context) is to also interrogate the ways that he/we have been seduced to believe that scholarship that is "good" (i.e., legitimate and worthy of consideration) has no relation to the body and spirit, is strictly of the mind, and then only of those minds that are not Black, female, or concerned with spirit. Such talk of the goodness in research requires the embrace of a universal notion of theory that ignores the influence of identity or history and totally dismisses consciousness of the body, of memory, of culture, of the way that all are also fundamentally implicated in any talk of theory (Busia, 1993; Darder, 2009; Madison, 2009; Hurtado, 2003). Such marshalling of theory as universal is, at its core, anti-feminist whenever we speak of theory as

> synonymous with "profound," "serious," "substantial," "scientific," "consequential," "thoughtful," or "thought-engaging"; and to any woman's ears, equivalent to "masculine," "hermetic," "elitist," and "specialized," therefore "neutral," "impersonal," "purely mental," "unfeeling," "disengaging," and—last but not least—"abstract." (Trinh, 1989, p. 41)

(Re)membering what we've forgotten as African ascendant women, through engaging cultural memories threatens the seduction of theory, upsetting the deeply rooted paradigms, theoretical notions, epistemologies and the taken-for-granted nature of the notion of theory itself. It decenters the talk of research and the theories that both drive it and that it generates, helping us to see clearly that what counts as "evidence" can also be unseen, spiritual, and is always cultural and embodied. For the person of African heritage, it is fundamentally a recognition that our theorizing and (re)membering also embodies a moral imperative, from an African cosmology (Ani, 1994; Battle, 2009; Dillard, 2010; Paris, 1995). These remembrances are what Armah (1973) refers to as our *way*, our cultural guidance and inheritance from the ancestors, deeply embedded in our cultural memories as African ascendant people. To be enticed to forget our way, Armah cautions, is to forget our very selves, to forget the wisdom that will both guide and save us:

> The teachers told us quietly that the way of experts had become a tricky way. They told us it would always be fatal to our arts to misuse the skills we had learned. The skills themselves were mere light shells, needing to be filled out with substance coming from our souls. They warned us never to turn these skills to the service of things separate from the way....Our way, the way, is not a random path. Our way begins from coherent understanding. It is a way that aims at preserving knowledge of who we are, knowledge of the best way we have found to relate each to each, each to all, ourselves to other peoples, all to our surroundings. If our individual lives have a worthwhile aim, that aim should be a purpose inseparable from the way....Our way is reciprocity. The way is wholeness. (Armah, 1973, p. 39)

And this is the crux of the seduction: To believe in a body of science and theories that have explicitly and purposefully manipulated African history and culture and the emotional and psychological well-being of an entire people (and others) is a seduction which continues to distort our humanity, encouraging detachment from ourselves, our histories and our spiritualities. But "the master's tools will never dismantle the master's house" (Lorde, 1984, p. 112): Our work is to bring our full selves (including our cultural memories) to bear witness *theoretically* on what constitutes "goodness" in science, using criteria that brave scholars have termed as decolonizing and indigenous (Dei, 2000, 2011; Smith, 1999); healing (Hull, 2001; King, 2005); conscious (Aristizabal & Lefer, 2010; Freire, 1970; Gutierrez, 2003; Hilliard, 1995), and spiritual (Dillard, 2006a; Fernandes, 2003, Strong-Wilson, 2008).

The scholar's question to me at the conference was also about scientific objectivity as the methodological goal of "good" science: It was clearly not a question arising from African feminist consciousness, where one raises questions to put under scrutiny (and possible erasure) the troubling notions of whose stories get told, when, where, and how. But what is most troubling is that what is deemed "good" in research is still a question that persists, continuing to marginalize women's voices and create what Trinh (1989) calls the "kingdom of the mute, the unreal and the 'illiterate'" (p. 57). What I am suggesting here is that, in order to (re)member, we must use our whole bodies, minds, and spirits as tools and sites to ask new questions of the goodness of science, of our multiple histories, of theory. These are questions that move far beyond Western pretenses of objectivity to a critical consciousness and awareness of life that has been previously silenced, forgotten, or dismissed entirely.

So to the brother-scholar above (and others open to considering their own interrogation of seductions), I would like to respond to his question with a few questions of my own:

1. How can an examination of spirituality and of memories be foreign or left out of discourses happening *within* an African context (Ghana) when spirituality is fundamental to the very understanding of African personhood, our epistemologies, our cultural production?

2. Why, among all of the scholars from the U.S. was there one only African American woman, given the number of African ascendant women scholars who talk about art, politics, and education? In what ways does this exclusion continue the silences that have surrounded Black women's ways of knowing and being in the world, particularly in the continental African context?

3. Given the theories that framed the majority of papers at the conference, how are patriarchal, anti-spiritual, anthropological and psychological theories reinscribing notions of inequity and injustice that have historically framed the work of research, particularly that which is done "on"/among Black people?

...ys are we, as African ascendant scholars, handicapped by our lack of ...wledge of our own cultural/theoretical production and histories and our embrace of the very theories that structure the systems of rewards in the academy that tend often not to see our contributions as "good" (as measured by becoming well known in elite academic circles, being published in top journals, etc.)?

5. In what ways does our inability to speak for ourselves through theoretical frameworks that honor Blackness in all its variations further frustrate our pursuit of a legitimate place at the table? Is that a pursuit worth pursuing at all?

6. Is there a way to think about "good" research as being something that actually helps African ascendants see more clearly the ways that we are intimately connected to and responsible for each other? In what ways can we see the *usefulness* of our research and theory production to our communities as a criterion of goodness?

I have many more questions. But the point is that asking these questions puts these very dangerous seductions of our humanity under scrutiny as well. As I (re)member my own wavering confidence in presenting my conference paper that day, I can see how deeply I too had been seduced into my own unworthiness, illegitimacy, and forgetfulness. But it's in the speaking that we find our voices. As we (re)member—body, mind, and spirit—we might be more able to resist these stereotypes and distortions and create new theories that are deeply grounded in Armah's (1973) call to (re)member the way. In these postmodern and multicultural times, some might be tempted to critique Armah's notion, of what appears to be a singular or dogmatic way (i.e., *the* way). But I would argue that from an endarkened feminist theoretical perspective, embodied in "the" is an ethos of African collectivity, an understanding of time as circular, a recognition that "the" includes the collective brilliance, experience, and wisdom of all who have lived, are living and will live. It is fundamentally our way of being in community, the "I" within the we. As Battle (2009) suggests (and I take up in Chapter 6), Armah's way can be characterized as an expansive "the," one that may keep those of African heritage from walking in the world as a flimsy copy of someone else's desires for us, enticing us to forget who we are and, in the process, encouraging us to (re)member *somebody else*. This is the seduction: To forget our stories and to (re)member those created *for* us:

> The point of view is the same: "Be like *us*"....Don't be us....Just be *like*, and bear the chameleon's fate, never infecting *us* but only yourself, spending your days muting, putting on/taking off glasses, trying to please all and always at odds with [my]self who is not self at all. (Trinh, 1989, p. 52)

Resisting this seduction of theory, we also resist alienation from ourselves as well as from history, from our memories as we've (re)membered them. Engaging cultural memories in our teaching and research endeavors, we also commit to a mutual and reciprocal process of recollection versus seduction: As we (re)member, we are also (re)membered within our communities, within frameworks that are communal, collective, and imbued with a greater consciousness of the places that "hold [y]our people to this earth" (McElroy, 1997, p. 2).

The seduction of the material over the spiritual world

A second seduction that is detrimental to African ascendant people and that can be resisted by engagements with cultural memory is that of privileging the material over the spiritual. In my first book, *On Spiritual Strivings: Transforming an African American Woman's Academic Life* (2006a), I explored in some depth the ways that our lives and work might be transformed by engagements with cultural memories, exploring questions and wonderings about spirituality and its usefulness in an academic life. And in a continuing quest to bring body, mind and spirit to bear in/on educational and social issues, one thing is clear: Considerations of spirituality in research and teaching can be both revelatory as well as revolutionary. However, too often we have come to believe that, like the pursuit of scientific objectivity and its many "rewards," it is only when something is observable and provable that we recognize and marshal it as "evidence," something that can be developed into theories of/in education, into research projects, and our whole lives. Seduced away from things spiritual, my own academic beginnings were filled with the seemingly appropriate yearning to become an excellent student of the mind, a student who gave precious little time to anything "spiritual." Like the brother-scholar at the conference, I came to understand that theorizing through something as invisible and unprovable as spirit could have very dangerous consequences, especially to an academic career. Who would publish my work? Who would see it as worthwhile, trustworthy, legitimate, "good"? So I too was seduced into believing that the more legitimate way to define myself as an intellectual (especially as an African American woman) was to embrace an identity that allowed access and validation (albeit very limited) to White folks' academic circles. Like so many, I'd been seduced into that dangerous chameleon-like state that Trinh (1989) spoke of earlier, one that I still see all too often in my students: Be like us, but never be us. What I can now name as the twin feelings of doubt and fear in presenting my conference paper that day also echo the outcomes of this seduction for African ascendant people.

> Such thinking, such behavior, such a belief system...is out of [seeking] consonance with white-male Western thinking which not only teaches dualism of the body and soul, but also elevation of the body over the soul. In a sense, then, I sought validation at the cost of my own soul. (Wade-Gayles, 1995, p. 3, emphasis mine)

This is the dilemma often faced by African ascendant women academics: How to embrace the cultural memories of our souls that arise from a spirituality that is the very fabric of Black life as we know it and how to do so within academic contexts that have little energy for the spiritual, especially as expressed by an African ascendant woman.

There are those who have also accurately suggested that the separation of mind and body has been a powerful strategy for survival for African ascendant people brutalized by histories of colonialism, slavery, Jim Crow, and persistent racism, sexism, and the cultural memories that are still unspeakable. For example, Christian (1985) takes up the issue of the mind and body duality and redefines the historical separation of mind and body for African American women, not in negative terms but in terms of survival "characterized not as fragmentation but as a source of wisdom" (p. 150). According to Rogers (2000), this separation was initially enabling for people of African heritage because, while our bodies might have been enslaved, we were able to determine our freedom by recalling Africa as the very source of our existence. However, from an African cosmology (and without the physical chains of slavery), I believe that the body and mind must not be torn asunder but instead examined for "what they productively reveal about the difficulties of negotiating autonomy in a racist (and I would add sexist) society" (Rogers, 2000, p. 78). Rogers further argues—and I agree— that it is within the contradictions, nuances, and diversities of cultural memories that a return to wholeness and consciousness is possible. Such consciousness is also an antidote to the persistence of the brother-scholar's question today, a question not unusual nor uncommon in academic circles for those who choose to (re)member that both the spiritual and material worlds are central to the work that we do, the lives that we live.

In many ways, the all encompassing nature of spirit and spirituality defies definition: It is all that is. However, I lean on Hull's (2001) definition here:

> Spirituality...involves conscious relationship with the realm of the spirit, with the invisibly permeating, ultimately positive, divine, and evolutionary energies that give rise to and sustain all that exists. (p. 2)

The key in this definition is that spirituality involves consciousness, involves choosing to be in relationship with the divine power and energy of all things. This is a powerful antidote against forgetting for African ascendant people, as it is fundamental to our history and the cultural memories that make up how we have been seen and been experienced and how we have seen and experienced ourselves as teachers, scholars, and persons in the world. And using this definition of spirituality, we might also see the theories within spirituality as a body of knowledge, as powerful frames from and through which to participate in the social and political struggles of the world.

But, what are the greater purposes of not privileging the material over the spiritual, of engaging spirituality and the evidence of things unseen as central and worthwhile educational pursuits for African ascendant people? As Madison (2009) points out, experiencing and theorizing through frameworks that include African cultural heritage knowledge, endarkened and Black feminisms, and respect for the body, mind, and spirit as containers of memory open possibilities of consciousness that move beyond the notion of goodness and against notions that rely solely on a scientism that, at its ontological and epistemological roots, denies the place of the body in the development of that consciousness. Implicated in African and endarkened frameworks, the body is part of our "evidence" against seductions. As Madison (2009) also points out:

> I am living evidence that this moment, this time and space, does exist and I am a surviving witness to its living realities of life and death and the infinite in-between....The body must testify, it must speak— it must provide a report—it must bear witness to the surfaces and the foundations, the symptoms and the causes. (p. 192)

Madison goes on to ask a profound question, one that I use here as provocation, as gesturing towards and providing direction for praxis that is possible in recollecting, reordering, and (re)membering, as African ascendants. Her question is this: *"What should I do with what I have witnessed?"* (p. 192). Related to cultural memories, what should I do with them beyond recalling the memory, feeling, and experience for the sake of the story alone? How might engaging our cultural memories lead us to respond to ourselves and the world differently, more humanely, with greater responseability? The following section points toward the answer.

Moving from seduction to praxis

The reverse of seduction involves developing consciousness, a sense of awareness of what's been forgotten, of what's worth (re)membering, and for what purposes. For African ascendant teachers and scholars and others whose history, cultural productions, knowledges, and theories have been relegated to the margins, it brings an additional duty to (re)member (Dillard, 2009), to (re)member our way (Armah, 1973).

It may be helpful here to recall the definition of cultural memory from a spiritual framework in order to remind us of the texture of the memories we are being asked to (re)member. First, cultural memories acknowledge an ever-present link between the diaspora and the cultural heritage, a heritage homeplace. Second, they are intimate, defining moments in life's histories, whether "good" or "bad," related to our "present "cultural identities. Finally, cultural memories influence our ways of knowing (epistemology) and our ways of being (culture) in what we call the present. So as Walker (1988) suggests, the process of engaging cultural memories might provide new connections and recognitions, new sites of accountability, and new sources of individual and collective power, a response to and possible reversal of the seductions that have enticed us from our righteous minds as African ascendant people. And the sort of vulnerability experienced in rejecting these seductions as an act of resistance and embracing knowledge, spiritual practices, memories, and ways of being that resonate with our bodies, minds, and spirits may take us to places that we've not "traveled," and sometimes to where we do not want to go. Couser (1996) describes the process of deeply engaging memories in relation to our race, ethnicity, and culture as being one in which

> Cocoonlike consciousness is repeatedly pierced by...distorting shards of the past....Unable to repress these elements any longer, *[we] learn to retrieve and reorder them in a purposeful way*...modeling ethnicity as a cultural production dependent on the creative labor of each generation for its perpetuation. (p.107, emphasis mine)

What Couser suggests is that (re)membering identity as praxis is not a static but rather a dynamic activity. It is voluntary, active and creative, kinesthetic, circular, and vital to a positive vision of African personhood. It is a process that allows each part of the body to become infused with consciousness (Trinh, 1989, p. 40). It involves examining the ways that one's cultural memories are dominated by various national even international narratives, memories that continue to deny value or usefulness to African history and cultural production whether on the continent of Africa or in the diaspora. For seductions to work, dominant ideologies must prevail in order to serve totalizing tendencies towards hegemony, to build memories (and memorials) that serve to create and define groups, including societies and nations (Booth, 2006). Hence, to be African ascendant people and to (re)member who we are can often be dangerous to the very notion of nationality (Singh, Skerrett, & Hogan, 1996). And the consequences can be very grave, including being labeled as un-American (or un-Canadian or fill-in-the-country's-name), metaphorically or literally exiled (whether from one's self collectively or from the national narrative and policies), or simply, as in the case of engaging in explicit scholarship of spirituality, of not seeing one's work as "good" enough.

It seems to me that learning to (re)member what we've forgotten—and the role of seduction in that forgetting—is about how one sees, evaluates, and records cultural memories of a collective of people connected by heritage and often common experience, and then explores and interrogates those cultural memories to also *create* culture, new ways of being out of the old. That is the consciousness, the wholeness called for here, what feminists of color have been advocating and exploring for years. (Re)membering and choosing from our rich inheritance of memory as African people to create and produce new culture that may serve to honor the soil from which it arises is the spirit of the way forward. It is a way not beholden to seduction but instead to creating our sense of the whole, of what's "good" in research and teaching. But such consciousness requires that we also be *ready* for wholeness, as Bambara cautions us all:

> *Are you sure you want to be well?...Just so's you're sure, sweetheart, and ready to be healed cause wholeness is no trifling matter, A lot of weight when you're well....Release, sweetheart. Give it all up. Forgive everyone everything. Free them. Free self.* (Bambara, 1980/1992, pp. 10–18)

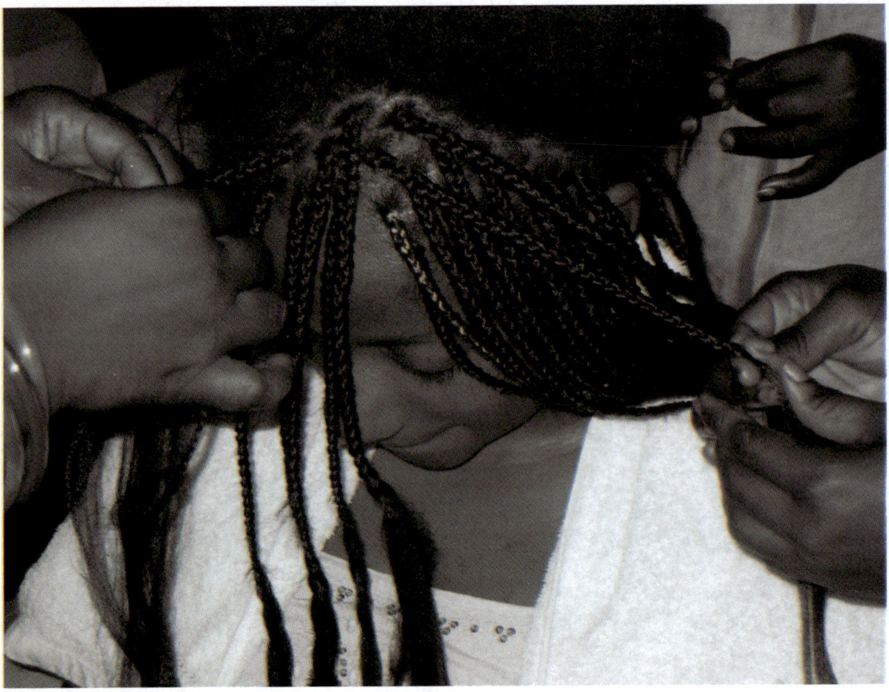

CHAPTER THREE

The Need to Love Blackness

Healing Cultural Memories of African Beauty

Loving Blackness

bell hooks writes the following dedication in her book *Black Looks: Race and Representation* (1992):

> I dedicate this book to all of us who love blackness, who dare to create in our daily lives spaces of reconciliation and forgiveness where we let go of past hurt, fear, shame and hold each other close. It is only in the act and practice of loving blackness that we are able to reach out and embrace the world without destructive bitterness and ongoing collective rage. (p. ii)

She has captured a fundamental and equally monumental task for African ascendant people generally and specifically for African ascendant teachers and researchers, that is, the recognition that our teaching and research arise from a coherent ideological and epistemological standpoint embedded in racial and cultural memories. I have pointed out in an earlier work that

> for most African ascendants who have been raised here in the United States, our definitions and identity, however powerful, have been developed against the backdrop of insidious racism, sexism, classism, and other "isms" that by their very nature are limiting, always about who we are *not* versus about who we are. These are not empowering realities. (Dillard, 2006a, p. 53)

So I'm suggesting that the practice of teaching and research for the teacher or researcher is to ask these epistemological and ideological questions of our own standpoints and identities: How those individual and collective experiences have influenced us and how these experiences live within us. Relatedly, we need to also ask ourselves: How do experiences live within those whom I study, with those whom I teach? What does culture mean for them? What does it look like? What are its notions and standards of beauty, of art? And as hooks (1992) asks: "From what political perspective do we dream, look, create, and take action?" (p. 4)

These questions gesture towards the notion of images: Those constantly swirling around us, those we have created within, those constructed about us. Images speak to the grand narratives and hegemony that have defined our realities as African ascendant women. And if we interrogate the ways that these images have too often deeply deformed the bodies, minds, and spirits of African ascendant women throughout the world, it is difficult to also deny that the predominant images of African women have an ideological intent. They are intended to influence and shape understandings of the nature of truth, notions of good or bad, right or wrong, desirable or undesirable. Further, these images are also epistemic: They have the ability to shape, move, and create realities. And one need only examine the evening news, the film industry (Ryan, 2005), many contemporary music videos, and fashion magazines to see the overwhelming misrepresentations and distortions depicted in the images of African women, given "a society full of institutionalized and violent hatred for both [our dark] skins and [our] female bodies" (Bethel, 1982, p.178). Just a few lines from Maya Angelou's (1990) powerful poem "Our Grandmothers" shows the outcomes of these degrading historical and contemporary images illustrated by the names too often assigned to African ascendant women. More importantly, it speaks of the tenacious and powerful ways that Black women throughout the world have resisted these negative images of our humanity...

> ...She heard the names swirling ribbons in the wind of history:
> Nigger, nigger bitch, heifer,
> Mammy, property, creature, ape, baboon,
> Whore, hot tail, things, it.
> She said, but my description cannot
> Fit your tongue, for
> I have a certain way of being in this world,
> And I shall not, I shall not be moved (p. 34)

The process Angelou describes of being subjects of degradation, of resisting degradation and of developing (through (re)membering) one's culture as a powerful ideological and epistemological standpoint is the focus of this chapter. I will explore, in a very intimate and personal way, what it means to (re)member (to productively put back together again) one's own "certain ways of being in the world," a standpoint that includes a coherent and loving image of our mothers, our names, our bodies, our ways of being as beautiful, and the ways such an inner vision might shape our teaching and research. It is an exploration that seeks to heal the "rips and tears at the seams of our efforts to construct self [and spiritual] identity" (hooks, 1992, p. 4). It's about laying down the impossibility of fitting into White, male, patriarchal, and downright false images of what we look like and who we are. It's about honoring the memories of our shared beauty and shared heritage as African women on the continent and in the diaspora. And for me and many other African ascendant women, one site of many possibilities in our healing process is about reconciling our images of and relationships with our hair and ultimately with our very souls...

> ...The image of a beautiful African woman walking tall and strong across thousands of miles we today call Europe is gloriously appealing. What was her name? Was she called Eve? Is it important what she was called? What would she feel if she returned today to find that some of her ancestors were enslaved, colonized, ethnically cleansed, subjected to rape, murder, holocausts, and reduced to impoverished masses, largely because they were assumed to be 'different'? With which mother's tears would she cry? What collective achievements or acts of love, kindness, compassion, sensuality, beauty, or creativity could we name that would bring a smile to her face? (Brah, 1999, p. 21)

I. Someone to watch over me: The braided beginnings

I was a cute Black child (or so my family thought). I had the requisite amount of hair, checked and rechecked over and over as an infant, fondled and brushed, and adorned with pink barrettes so that no one would ever think to mistakenly identify me as a boy. I, on the other hand, hated my hair, preferring the silky blondness of my White Barbie doll's hair instead. Being one of four girls in my family, I think my mother hated my hair too. She often referred to it as "nappy" and "hard," "difficult," and "dull." And I had a head FULL of it! While braids were the rage for little girls in the 60s, I think braiding was really my mother's way of tightly reining in the wildness of the hair on my head, of not letting it be "loose." And not being loose was one of the prime lessons we learned as young Black girls growing up in Seattle, Washington (mostly by listening to grown folks conversations). Reining it in was her way of watching over me.

My parents took lots of pictures of me when I was little girl, with an antique camera that my dad held near his waist and looked down into. But in every childhood photograph, I am frowning. I wonder now if it had to do with my braided beginnings and the struggles I knew would come as I wrestled with my hair. In reflection, that wrestling was not really with my hair at all: It was a tug-of-war I was having with myself.

II. "Say it loud (if it won't offend anybody): I'm Black and I'm proud!"

By the mid-1970s, my hair was saying something else, itself singing the Black anthem of the times: "Say it loud, I'm Black and I'm proud!" Angela Davis had become my role model. Black had become my favorite color (even though my mother said that girls shouldn't wear "that" color: Pastels were so much more "appropriate"). So, while I couldn't wear the color black, I made up for it with big Angela-wannabe hoop earrings that I bought with my own money from my retail sales job at the mall. And as this emerging sense of Black identity was coming into consciousness on my head, there was a little spark of Black consciousness rising inside me, too. I learned that some people (White and Black alike, for different reasons) were afraid to say or to hear "it" too loud. I learned that the mere mention of Malcolm X either at home or at school caused many adults to sputter words about him being crazy or too radical or "getting what was coming to him." At school, the teacher quickly dismissed my query about reading the *Autobiography of Malcolm X* during Black History week: "We will read about Martin Luther King. He's a much more appropriate role model for a young Negro girl like you," she smiled. While I would later come to see such persons as blatantly racist, I do think she was in the category that Naomi Wolf (1995) calls WMWP: Well-meaning White people (p. 44).

But by the end of the 1970s, times weren't the only thing that changed. Chemically relaxed and permed hair, the kind that mimicked (often poorly) the Farrah Fawcett image on *Charlie's Angels* was the prevailing hairdo. And given the naps that the Lord had blessed me with, I had to work very hard to emulate this style. And it wasn't just the hair that I was working to get: It was all the accoutrements of Whiteness that went with it. My wish? "If I could only say words the way they (White people) say them." And while their language was never as alive in my ears as the Black speech was at home, that did not dampen my desire to acquire its 'proper' cadence and sound. And given that the American literature we were required to read were only classics in the European sense, Shakespeare never quite sounded right when I dropped the "g's," ran parts of the sentences together, or added an inflection that tried to make it sound like my auntie, who fancied herself a second Maya Angelou. Never mind that Malcolm and Angela Davis were still a shadowy part of my existence, a sort of youthful Black background that I had now pushed down, somewhere deep inside me. Farther and farther down with every box of Dark and Lovely relaxer. Farther and farther down, with every minute that the relaxer burned the shit out of my scalp. Farther and farther with every scab that rose in protest to this ongoing violence and control that I was convinced would be my deliverance and acceptance into what I know now is an ideological, cultural, and aesthetic politic that does not judge the African essence of a sister like myself to be beautiful.

Underneath my now-processed hair, I was in serous doubt and serious fear, afraid of my own African-ness and what it would mean in the world. Could I keep this White boyfriend of mine without straightening and taming these naps? I mean, he'd tolerated this hair of mine for years, even occasionally saying it was pretty. But his preference *must* have always been something more akin to his own, right? What would other folks think? I'd never get a job or into a decent university unless I looked presentable (read: As close to White as a sister could get), right?

Doubt and fear are a trip. They keep you constantly on edge, never knowing for real who or what you are. But more importantly, they keep you wondering what you really are in the world.

III. Living the contradiction: "Relaxed" hair

undecided conjugations, 1993

should i?
shouldn't i?
can i?
can't i?
do i?
don't i?
could i?
couldn't i?
am i?
aren't i?
would i?
wouldn't i?
will i?
won't i?
why?
why not?

Interlude

You see, Black people's hair began where human life began: In Africa. However for African Americans and others in diaspora, exploring and transforming racial and cultural memories of one's *natural* hair, given the history of slavery, oppression, and the hegemony of European standards of beauty, is a radical movement against assimilation, an embrace of an African aesthetic, of Blackness and ethnicity, of solidarity with Africa and the diaspora. Further, African culture has always utilized the body for expression, and the head (and by extension, the hair) as a site and source of physical and spiritual well-being. One constant that African ascendant women share, relative to hair, is its social, cultural, and historical significance and its relation to notions of beauty and worth (Byrd & Tharps, 2001). And part of what we feel in relation to hair is a *spiritual* connection. But make no mistake: Spiritually probing the depths of notions of beauty and aesthetic from an endarkened feminist perspective is healing work, mining the depths of one's racial and cultural memories for what they can produce in the "present." For the teacher and researcher, this is also the work of healing teaching and research methodologies in ways that push them towards being situated, sacred, and spiritual, methods that ask us to question how we are seen and how we see ourselves, methods that happen in multiple spaces and places where African ascendants and other indigenous people find ourselves.[1]

IV. I'm coming out: The first missionary phase

The Missionary Phase began when I was an undergraduate at a rural small college in the Pacific Northwest: Central Washington University. It's the phase where I learned some of the most profound lessons about the meaning of Blackness, manifest in my continuing struggles with my hair. First, I tried to keep the relaxer going with absolutely no Black hairdressers and no access to the relaxer kits to even try to do it myself! So like my sisters before me, I was always rockin' scarves and hats in those final weeks prior to going home 'cuz the comb couldn't find its way through my hair! Doubt and fear continued to be a big part of my life at this time, but differently, as I began to experience an overt, hostile racism that I had not experienced in my multicultural growing up in Seattle. My strategy? Load up on credits each quarter so that I could get the hell out of that hostile place *alive*! But no matter how overloaded I was with credit hours, I could not outrun the resurgent Ku Klux Klan on the campus. And these encounters were not on the big screen, a figment of my imagination, or mentioned in some history book: They were upclose and personal. And the Klan taught me a lot about just how powerful Black women really *are*, simply because we *exist*. As a way to deal with the rage I still feel some three decades later, I have written this letter to the Klan as a way to work through this cultural memory of my encounters and to reconcile these remembrances in the present…

Dear KKK members,

I want you to know something. I heard the names that you called me. I felt your spit on my sleeve. I felt your hot breath all up in my face. I felt and still feel today the sharp toes of your shoes. I watched you terrorize those right-thinking White folks in whose store I worked. And you know what? I indeed "learned my lesson." But I don't think it was the lesson you intended. You see, when you worked that hard to define me, to do violence to me, and ultimately (you hoped), to strike fear in me, I realized at that moment, that there was some kind of power in being a Black woman. And that power could be evoked simply by gazing upon me, upon my Black body. That's some kind of power!!! So I took that Black woman body power and I added some knowledge kind of power (yea, I'm now one

---

[1] Questions are often raised about authenticity and definitions of Indigenous, who belongs and who does not. In that spirit, indigeneity describes the knowledge, values, and practices of Indigenous groups, particularly those with contemporary roots in African culture that are honored, nurtured and valued in contemporary times. We lean on Hilliard (1995) who defined African Indigenous teachers/scholars as "selfless healer[s], intent on inspiring, transforming and propelling students to a higher spiritual level" (pp. 69–70).

of those educated Black people who knows my place to be higher education and yep—even sometimes in the Dean's Office), and I added some feminist/multicultural/and radical activist power, and I called up the power of courage, humility, and Spirit passed on by the ancestors, and, you know what? I intend, as Mari Evans says to "spit in the mouths of the babies" (and my babies are teachers who are teaching YOUR babies)! I will teach them all the lessons you helped me learn so that these teachers and their students never, ever, forget that you still exist, even as you return again and again, disguised in a different set of "sheets." Thank you. I can now stand up and say with a confidence and power I would have never had before: I AM AN AFRICAN AMERICAN WOMAN TEACHER WILLING TO EMBRACE ALL OF ME FOR THE GOOD OF ALL OF US. You might want to be careful when you tell someone to "learn their lesson" from some hateful things that you've done: Often those wishes come true. Ashe!...

Because there were very few other Black folks on the campus, most of my friends were White. It was a personal and social crisis when I began to wonder to myself: Was that my friend so-and-so under that white sheet?

V. The second missionary phase

Missionary Phase 2 was a very long phase in my life. I finally said f— it to trying to be something I wasn't and cut every hair on my head completely off! It was a sort of nakedness, a vulnerability that screamed to the world: "*This is me just as I am.*" I was learning that my body and my skin would always tell a different story than the stories often swirling around me. They would tell a sort of truth, a story I was learning to live as a natural woman (thanks, Aretha). It was a period when I stopped pretending that I was a person interested in earning a lot of money through a career in fashion, sales, and marketing and followed my heart, working out my fashion jones by wearing gorgeous adornments and African clothing that gestured at what was underneath. Instead, I began to embrace the work that had brought me so much joy: Teaching. But even with my new short hair, I still felt as Alice Walker (1988) said: "Something inside me seemed to be waiting, holding its breath, unsure about what the next step should be [to] eventually becoming the person I wish for, a new phase of [my] life" (p. 71). And after nearly 16 years with my cropped style, I realized that another barrier to my cultural, ideological, and spiritual liberation might still rest in my hair. Just because it was natural in texture didn't mean that shaving it nearly all off wasn't another missionary solution, a way of controlling it, keeping it "*acceptable*," "*reining*" it in. My hair just simply wanted to grow and to be left alone to do so. And, at forty years of life, that's what I finally let it do: I locked my hair.

VI. My spiritual antenna

With every embrace of an African aesthetic, the African in this American gets stronger and stronger. And during this process, it also seemed that many of my dreams were coming true, as I built and grew, lived and learned, deeply influenced by the people and culture in Ghana, West Africa. I realized I needed and loved the extra allure and strength that natural hair and now my locks gave to me. Not natty dreads, the sort that signify a person as Rastafarian, my brothers and sisters in the spirit of I-and-I. I simply called these i'll-do-as-i-please hairs on my head *locks*, representing a way to be natural and still just a little "reined" in: I wanted to be able to step foot in my momma's house, you know!

But what was important to me was that my locks signified more than my nearly shaved head did: They signified a commitment to uncompromised African-ness. And unlike those who saw them simply as fashion, I did wear them for political reasons, particularly in an academy that often attempted to deny my existence as a Black woman. But I wore them for spiritual reasons, too: They felt like antenna with a direct link to the Creator, who told me through each and every one of them that all was well. And they were an *African* style. As one of my locked brothers, Vernon Reid, in the gorgeous book called *Dreads* (1999) said: "Fashion may be momentary. But style as an expression of self is never shallow" (p. 103).

That's why I couldn't call my locks dreadlocks. How could anything so beautiful, so absolutely splendid even begin with the word "dread"? My locks also reminded me that being educated was all about getting rid of language that denigrated my Self and others like me. Words like "minority," and "theory" and "enlighten." How about "majority," "motherwit" and "endarken"? Naming creates identity: It matters deeply how I refer to my Self and how I refer to my hair and other things I care about, as the language we use tells a deeper truth about our lives and our relationships to life.

Oh, but there were new issues that other people had with the choices I'd made to lock my hair. The women in the village of Mpeasem, Ghana (where I am enstooled Queen Mother of Development[2]) found my hair so difficult! Their words were reminiscent of my mother's, as they wrapped me in kente cloth for my enstoolment ceremony: "What

---

2 In order to become Queen Mother of Development, a woman is chosen for this role by the Chief and Elders of the Village and has the responsibility for developing the Village. A formal ceremony is held in the Village where the woman takes an oath of allegiance to the Chief. Her stool, selected by the Elders to symbolize her character through the Adinkra symbol carved into the stool, is brought to the ceremony. She doesn't immediately sit on the stool but is made to take two "tries" at sitting. On the third try, she finally sits on her stool and is thus, *enstooled*. While the stool of the Queen Mother of Development is not required to be given through matrilineal or clan affiliation, an enstooled Queen Mother serves as a leader of the village, alongside the Chief and Elders, for life.

should we do with it?" they decried. Or the young folks in Ghana who went out of their way to call after me: "Rasta! One love!" But these are the same brothers who also too often assumed that smoking weed was my favorite pasttime. Or folks who wanted to remind me of how "dirty" they had always assumed locks were. Or those sisters who, not understanding our 400 years without a comb, just couldn't figure out how I "got [my] hair like that" (or worse yet, assumed that like they had done, I just bought and attached it). These were often the same sisters who would wonder (OUT LOUD!) about acceptability, about how "different" locks were to (European) standards of beauty. But what they were really talkin' about was their own discomfort, as if I had exposed some secret about them. What I wanted to do was scream out loud: "Hello! Black people are not White people who just happen to be black, just as Black hair/African hair is not White hair regardless of the chemicals we apply to it or how much of it we weave onto our heads! Our hair is typically tightly coiled and responds naturally to the elements. In other words, it will go back to the Motherland in a heartbeat! But the more time I spend in Africa, the more I realize what a blessing this hair is to me: It (re)*members*. It puts back together the missing and broken pieces of my lives—those lived before, the one that I am living now, and those soul-travelings that I'll do as an ancestor. It reminds me that the notions of independence, of existing solely as individuals are really European notions. As African people, whether in hair or in survival, we know deeply the importance of tight support, of bonding, much like the locks did on my head, tips red from the strength of the Ghanaian sun. And every day, through every lock on my head, God told me so.

VII. From the inside out: Being peace

I'm in my mid-50s now and blessed year round with my own personal summers. But as the bumper sticker on my office door reads: *These are not hot flashes: They are power surges!* Two years ago, I was in Ghana, leading a retreat, with 12 amazing African American women from all walks of life. And my eighteen-year-old niece Taylor was one of two young sisters who kept us all physically moving throughout the trip: soccer, volleyball, jogging: You name it, they were ready to play it! On one of our free days, the young ones had organized everyone for swimming, something that I love to do. "Oh, but wait," I said to myself. "My locks will get wet and in the Ghanaian humidity, they won't dry well." And moldy locks were nothing to be desired! But wanting desperately to feel myself in the water, I coiled my locks in a big beehive on top of my head and joined the others. But that day, I really didn't "swim" but cautiously moved through the pool with my head above water, being careful not to get my hair wet. And the contradiction was too much for me! My own thoughts and actions now echoed those of my mother, who continually threatened us not to sweat or swim or do anything related to water and our hair. Wasn't the reason I had natural hair to be free of imposed limits? It was a crystallizing moment for my spirit and my hair. After more than 10 years (and nearly 10 pounds) of locked hair that I loved deeply and that had loved me back, I let go of my locks. While it was easy for me to cut them, doing so caused great despair for many who loved my "long" hair. But this time, I recognized their angst as the same Barbie doll image reappropriated with natural hair: It was about cutting off *long* hair [read: Hair that had reached lengths seldom possible for those addicted to what Chris Rock (in Stilson, 2010) calls the "creamy crack"]. But for me? There was no drama, no questions, no regrets: It was simply time for the locks to go and I knew it way down in that space where spirit resides. But interestingly, the stiff necks, backaches, and pain that had unknowingly crept into my body, creating tension where it didn't exist before were also gone.

The next year, I made my annual sojourn to Ghana again. But this time, rockin' a short Afro, I felt *free*. The sort of freedom that comes from *within*, from seeing that my life's wrestlings with my hair were all about finding my way back home: To *my* spirit and *my* being beautiful on *my* terms. And it had been a great year: Spirit had blessed me with abundance untold.

So what is beautiful now? A deeper realization that African women, in all of our differences, are the beauty we seek. Alice Walker (1984) speaks of her love of horses and how they "make the landscape more beautiful." I think Black women make the landscape more beautiful as well. And my time in Ghana has helped to shape new criteria and standards of beauty that too few Africans in the diaspora have yet experienced, one that is against a backdrop that is Black, that is African. Sisters wearing colors that our diasporan mothers have told us for generations are not for us. Sisters whose substantial backsides mirror my own and who unabashedly don slit skirts designed to emphasize what one sister called "the blessing God gave us." Young sisters whose weave-ons and wigs are not adornments but a serious commitment to creating and (re)creating a "new" African aesthetic, drawing from and blending cultural elements from around the world in new terms, often arising from pieces of the old. Our hair, historically referred to as our crowning glory, is symbolic of our deep well of cultural memories that go far beyond the seduction of Whiteness as the desirable standard of beauty. In those memories lies an aesthetic whose standard is at once cosmopolitan (Appiah, 2006), "African" (in all its variations and possibilities) and multiple "composed, not of one, but of many peoples [whose] origins are not singular, but diverse (Hall, 1999, p. 5). Such cultural memories are powerful not simply because we are connected to a "common" African heritage "but because of how we have gone about producing 'Africa' again…" (p. 13), through our memories and imaginaries:

> Equally significant, then is the way this 'Africa' provides resources for survival today, alternative histories [memories] to those imposed by colonial rule, and the raw materials for reworking in new and distinctive cultural patterns and forms. (p. 13)

Hall goes on to say that many movements (Civil Rights, Black feminism, Rastafarianism, to name a few) have represented themselves as a 'return' to culture, a return to ways of being and knowing cultural production, including our notions of what it means to be/see/produce beauty, particularly for African ascendant women. He argues that these movements of return, like the cultural memories embedded in our hair, produce and enable a transformation in both the nature of knowledge and our ability to (re)member ourselves (individually and collectively) in new and important ways:

> ...what [movements of return] 'returned' to us was *ourselves*. In doing so, [they] produced 'Africa' again—in the diaspora....Culture is not just a voyage of rediscovery, a return journey....Culture is a production. It has its raw materials, its resources, its 'work-of-production.' It depends on knowledge of tradition as the changing same...But what this 'detour through its pasts [its cultural memories] does is to enable us, through culture, to produce ourselves anew, as new kinds of subjects. It is therefore not a question of what our traditions make of us so much as *what we make of our traditions*. (pp. 15–16, emphasis mine)

While I will take up in more detail the power of (re)membering traditions and rituals in Chapter 4, what Hall is advocating can be seen as an expansive and expanded notion of culture. Like my signifyin' hair, it requires a shift from forgetting African women's beauty to recreating and (re)membering African women's beauty as feminist praxis in research and teaching. But as Gilroy (1993) suggests, it is also possible to see African women's identity (and beauty) "as a process of movement and meditation" (p. 19). And a meditation, by definition, "cannot presuppose answers or conclusions" (Brah, 1999) but rather creates a space for insights to arise, for a dialogue to be possible both within one's spirit and across our differences. Fundamentally, loving Blackness for the African ascendant is a process where we must tell the truth of our lives as we have lived them, individually and as a part of the collectives that have shaped our ability to both forget and (re)member. Seeing our selves as "daughters of deep memory" (Jackson-Opoku, 1997, p. 83) might enable us to seek new ways to think, feel, love and create a spirit of Blackness on our own terms and for our own purposes...

> Our history is a cowrie with both an outer shell and a hidden heart. Unless you know both sides you stumble in the present and blunder in the future...I see the story, my people, from the inside out. (Jackson-Opoku, 1997, p. 22)

Beauty from the inside out is the legacy and standard of beauty we need for ourselves and for our children: African. Connected. Collective. Creative. Whole. And Beauty-full.

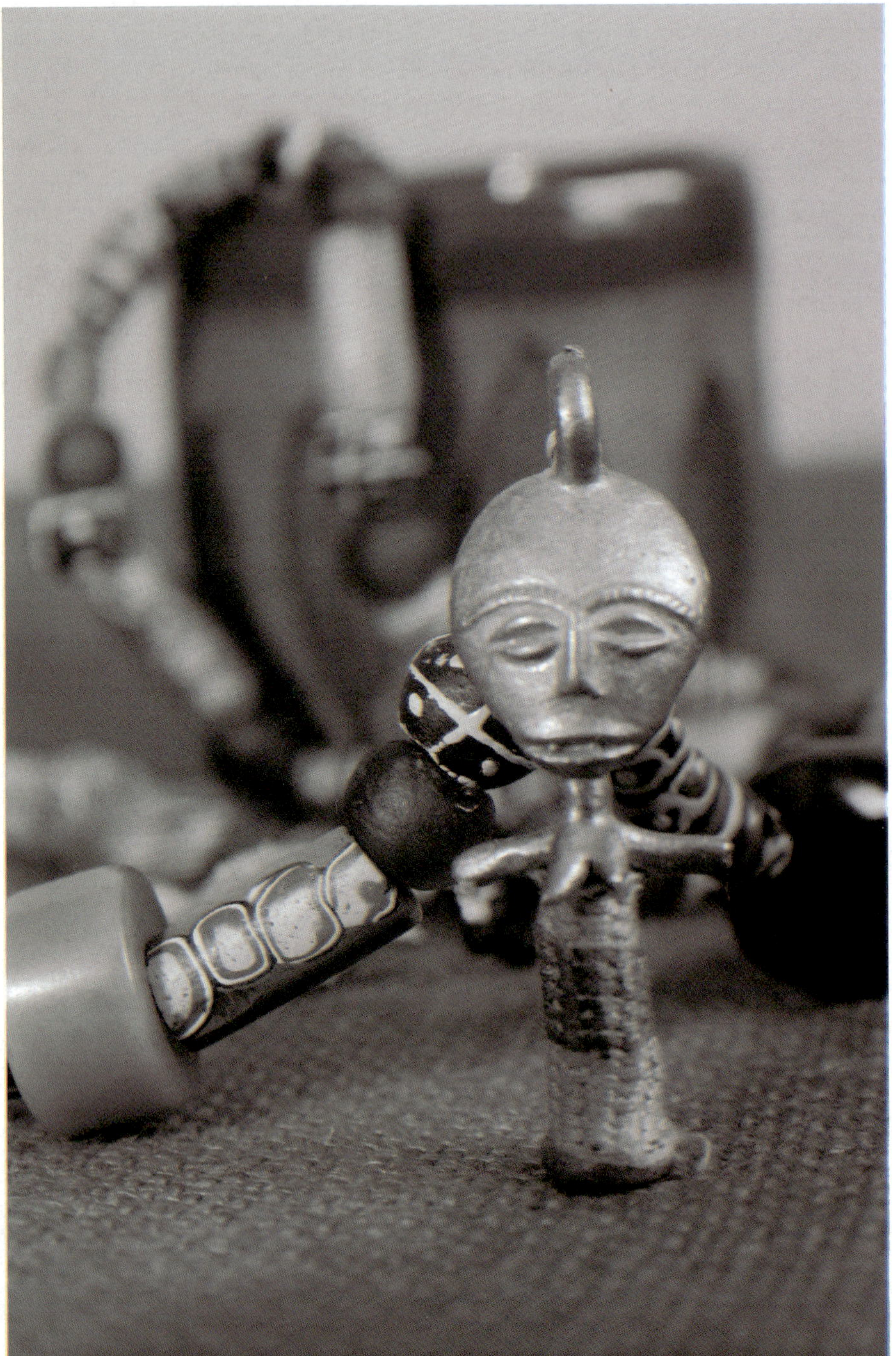

CHAPTER FOUR

The Power of Rituals and Traditions

(Re)membering African Culture, (Re)membering African Knowledge

> You see this basket holds beads of many sorts and sizes, as delicate as drops of water. Some more complex and intricate than any spider's design. I collect them as our daughters enter this village and deposit their waist beads at death's gate. If you look closely you can discern within each bead the hues of blues; this woman's birth, that one's budding of breasts; the first blood, the sacrament of sex, childbearing, old age, death. Feel their surfaces, the ridges of happiness and hollows of heartbreaks. Hear in them as they meet each other, the sound of living waters. (Jackson-Opoku, 1997, p. 11)

In her award-winning book, *The River Where Blood Is Born*, Sandra Jackson-Opoku uses beadwork to describe the act of stringing together the rich history and memory of African people: Of time and location, of important moments and rites of passage, of birth, death, and the spiritual nature of experience and culture. The notion of beadwork both literally and as a metaphor (Lakoff & Johnson, 1980) is useful in describing the power and central place of ritual and traditions for African people. I have come to see handmade beads as containers and symbols of cultural memory helpful in examining questions of identity, spirituality, knowledge, subjectivities, and the complexity of African cultural production. As such, there are several characteristics of beads that are important to marshalling beads as a metaphor for cultural memory.[1] First, like cultural memory, beads are also *cultural*, imbued with deep and sacred meanings to the wearer and of the beads themselves as adornments. They are also relatively small in size, which aids in their movement and influence from culture to culture. However, each bead tells a deeper story of the culture and the history of the people who created it, the relationships between peoples and how it traveled from place to place. As containers of memory, they are a beautiful reminder of the cultural nature of life all over the world.

Second, beads, like cultural memories are multisensory. They are containers of memory that are embodied, that engage, body, mind, and spirit. In other words, like memory, you can hear, touch, see, smell, taste, and feel them in and with the body. For African ascendant women, they represent what Oyewumi (2005) describes as our

---

[1] The following summary of the characteristics of beads is adapted from a lecture by Joyce Griffiths, former owner of Byzantium Beads in Columbus, OH. While I've added some embellishments, her framework is helpful in thinking about the importance of beads and bead making in the world.

world sense. The distinction here is that the European notion of worldview is too narrow, not taking into account the multiplicity of ways of knowing beyond what can be seen (i.e., world "view"). Within African ways of knowing, Oyewumi argues one knows not only through what one can see but also through what one hears, touches, feels, intuits, taking into account the spiritual nature of our senses, the evidence of things unseen.

Third, beads as containers of memory can unite and identify a group but can also distinguish the role of the wearer (for example, chiefs, queens, etc.). Fourth, as bearers of cultural memories, beads can be useful, for example in measurement and counting time, space, weight, like an abacus or an Ashanti brass piece. Fifth, beads as containers of memory are spiritual, often used for prayers and protection (in Buddhist, Hindu, Muslim, and Catholic spiritual traditions, for example). Finally, beads are art and are also used to create art: As in memories, they are both individual and collective. And like the African feminist notions of beauty discussed in the previous chapter, beads contain their own history and mystery: They are beauty and art on their own terms. Together, they create the art of the bead, something that we can treasure, love, and pass on to others. And as Madam Felicia Ayertey says: "The bead is constant always. It is an inheritance from our fathers and the children should learn that" (Wilson, 2003, p. 89).

Beads as containers of cultural memory also can describe the spiritual location of memory and the multiple locations of (re)membering ritual and tradition for African people in diaspora. Certainly, many scholars have described the complexities of fragmentation, dislocation, and the challenges of living African heritage within and against our connected and collective diasporic locations (Busia, 1989; Dillard, 2006a; Du Bois, 2005/1940; Hall, 1999; King, 2005; Marshall, 1984). Equally important, however, is to examine those memories and traditions that also *hold culture together*. When creating a strand of beads or a necklace, a person must have something on which to place and string the beads, often silken thread, cord, sinew, elastic, or chain. But whatever the "thread," without it, the beads remain simply unconnected raw material. Separate. Individual. Fragmented. Often able to simply roll away. So, it stands to reason that if we envision beads as individual containers of memory, the more beads we (re)member (i.e., gather and put together, in relation to/with one another), the more beautiful, full and expansive might be our collective strand, our collective memory. One might think of the material that holds these beads of memory together as *ritual*, a central "thread" or activity woven across locations, histories and through time, ripe with the wisdom to (re)member ourselves and our work on this human journey.

Ritual, as a thread for (re)membering within African community

[is] culturally both religious and social in origins and purpose. It keeps the whole community of the living and the dead united and keeps all the forces of life in harmony for another season. The ancestors are remembered for their continuing protection, and failing to keep their memory alive leads to the destruction of the community…[They] are the physical representation of those metaphysical silken threads… [making] the link across waters and boundaries of generation and time. (Busia, 1989, pp. 208–210)

Further, ritual is "the yardstick by which people measure their state of connection with the hidden ancestral realm" (p. 12). So ritual does not simply refer to a particular or singular act like saying a prayer, a reciprocal sacrifice, or mysteriously speaking in tongues: That is too often the common understanding in contemporary popular culture. Rather, from an African spiritual perspective, it describes the necessity of a deeper recognition of everyday acts as life affirming, lived in honor of the inheritance of the ancestors and the legacy of which we are a part as African ascendant people. So while ritual may certainly include offering prayer, engaging in meditation, eating together, enacting sacrifice, or other redemptive acts, I use it here to describe *a way of living* that is fundamentally about making space for consistent recognition of our spiritual and cultural inheritance as African people. Not superfluously, but *consciously*. Paule Marshall provides a poignant example in her description of the protagonist Avey's painful recognition of what she and her husband Jay lost in succumbing to the seduction to forget the rituals and celebrations that had provided them with a sense of African American culture, of their own power in a hostile and racist world, and of the essence of their cultural inheritance, their "beads":

> Something in those small rites, an ethos they held in common, had reached back beyond her life and beyond Jay's to join them to the vast unknown lineage that had made their being possible. And this link, these connections, heard in the music and in the praisesongs of a Sunday: '*I bathed in the Euphrates when dawns were/young….,*' had both protected them and put them in possession of a kind of power. All this had passed from their lives without their hardly noticing…*Too much!* They had behaved, she and Jay, as if there had been nothing about them worth honoring….(Marshall, 1984, pp. 137 and 139, emphasis hers)

Seen from an endarkened feminist space, a ritual approach to our teaching and research practice would also honor the wisdom, spirituality, and critical interventions of transnational Black woman's ways of knowing and being in cultural and collective memory, stringing the spiritual and the material beads of African women together, from African continent to diaspora and back again. Rituals would include those that affirm a consciousness of the realm of the spirit in our everyday lives, those that recognize such consciousness as a transformative force in research and teaching work, and those that lift up the work as *sacred*, as worthy of being held with reverence as it is done (Dillard & Okpalaoka, 2011). And fundamentally, teaching and research that affirm the place of ritual for African ascendant people would centrally be about finding "the answers to the questions of origins before [we] can return home [to ourselves]" (Busia, 1989, p. 205).

The challenge of living and reading the African diaspora is not an easy one: Our beads and our rituals have been lost, stolen, renamed, reappropriated, buried, and crushed without regard under the boots of many. They have been left out, torn asunder. They are sometimes difficult to recognize, even for African people ourselves. What would it take to read the diaspora, to research through our memories of rituals, questions of identity, place, and sacred knowledge of African traditions?

I turn again to Marshall's *Praisesong for the Widow* (1984) as an example of and tribute to the ritualized (re)membering of an African American woman. This text is a potential and powerful road map we might follow in the process of (re)membering ourselves as African ascendants. In the book, as Avey (re)members, through uncovering and arduously bringing to meaning and consciousness what she's forgotten, she symbolically reverses the journey of the transatlantic slave trade and its consequent diaspora to one that *ends* in Africa (vs. in the Americas). This return to consciousness—through her encounters with various rituals, songs, dances, sights, and experiences spanning locations in the U.S. and the Caribbean—reinvests Africa with worth and meaning to Avey: The process returns to her some of the African cultural beads that she tried desperately throughout her life to take off, to throw aside, to be seduced not to wear. I mention this work of fiction to make an important point: To see one's self as African can return to our consciousness both memories and rituals of personal and collective community for which we might more productively envision, read, and reproduce cultural identities and inheritances as African ascendant women in new ways. These stories are production of African culture, the stringing together of old and new beads to create something new. Drawing on fragments of tradition in this process, we might be able to interpret and to tell new and meaningful stories of Africa, the African, of the "fact of Blackness" (Fanon, 1967, p. 109), and answer the question "What is Africa is to me?" (Soyinka, 1999, p. 145). Busia (1989) says this:

> Storytelling, including the telling of [our] own story…in progress…must be undertaken within a cultural [and spiritual] context, a context that includes, as indexes in the composition of [the] story, aspects such as dress, food, dance and formal and informal ritual, in addition to the words themselves. It is not only the story itself which has meaning but the circumstances of its telling.… (p. 200)

For the teacher or researcher engaged in ritualizing the methods and practices that we use, Busia's words characterize an endarkened feminist framework involving several engagements for both ourselves and our students. First of all, we must be drawn into and conscious of the place of spirit, the inner place in our lives where spirit resides. Second, we must be engaged with/in relevant cultural rituals, people, spaces, and places (in this case, of Africa and her diaspora) in intimate and authentic ways in our teaching and learning. Finally, we must be open to being transformed by all that is encountered and recognize such encounters as spiritually guided and purposeful, with the potential to expand our vision and being. Such engagements will certainly expose us to stories not our own, that may sometimes even seem incredible to our minds and hearts. However, such engagement *requires* us to bear witness to both beads and threads, memories and rituals strange and familiar, new and old, maybe all at once. And these beads are wise, they come to teach us lessons. For *"When a daughter makes a conscious effort to connect with our wisdom, that is when an ancestor mother must reach out a helping hand."* (Jackson-Opoku, 1997, p. 227, emphasis mine)

Beads of Wisdom: Stringing 101

Lesson #1: (Re)membering our beads make us more aware of the worth of our being, of what spirit calls us to do.

A few years ago, I was walking through the Pike Place market area in Seattle, enjoying the sights and the sounds of my hometown. Unexpectedly, from around the corner, came the incredible smell of incense. I followed this amazing scent, ending in a little metaphysical store on the corner, full of books, candles and meditation supplies. I was met by a lovely woman at the counter who suggested that I have a (psychic) reading with a person she described as an "amazing visionary" and who was available at the time. Curious but a bit skeptical, I decided to see him, as I had a lot of important decisions to make in my academic and personal life at the time: Maybe he could tell me something that I didn't already know? I waited for a bit, and then was ushered through a beaded screen into a waiting area where I met Dariusz. A small, rather bookish-looking man with a mess of brown hair and delicate wireframed glasses, the energy about him was palpable. The two of us entered a small room where, with an eagle feather in his hand, he cleared the room, my aura, and his own, all the while offering a prayer to the spirits of nature and the universe for the visions and truth that would heal me and the world.

The spirits told me many things through Dariusz, including in a beautifully innocent way, of my father's and sister's impending deaths within 10 days of one another. They/He spoke of my dreams of building a retreat center and schools in Ghana and how my work as a teacher was also the work of healing the profession of teaching.

Then he stopped, tilting his head as if listening to a very important message being whispered into his ear. "This is an exquisite vision you have. Do you hear? Spirits are very pleased. Stop worrying about how it will happen and just get the goddamn work done!" Impressed by his seeming irreverence as a spiritual man (and encouraged by it as well), I relaxed a bit, as he specifically went on to talk about my role as a Queen Mother in Mpeasem, Ghana. About how I'd been chosen a queen long before I was enstooled as one. And then he turned to stare at a strand of layered beads that I was wearing, one of my favorites from Ghana. "You have to learn to be like the beads you love, like hollow bones," he said. "Solid, but open in the center, allowing Spirit Energy to flow through freely. Surrender to that openness. Be your authentic African woman self, as full and as beautiful as the beads. Quit hiding and listening to other people's talk and opinions. Listen to that circle of Energy inside of you. That is where your wisdom lives. Let it be so." I was only able to visit this very talented visionary one more time before he unexpectedly made his transition to the other world the following year.

Lesson #2: (Re)membering our beads reminds us to be vigilant, to safeguard our ways of being and knowing.

Sunday, January 6, 2008

Dear Sisters of the Yam:[2]

I left yesterday's gathering so inspired! And it seems to me that, given the connections and conversations that we had (and those to come), hooks's notion of being Sisters of the Yam fits us too. Sisters who are about the business of healing. And naming ourselves/group "Sisters of the Yam" also allows us to have a substantive and personal relationship with ourselves regardless of our place on the globe. That feels good. I feel like we are on the cusp of something bigger than we may even imagine! I say that because, as Chineze suggested, there is very little in the education literature about sisters (or African ascendant people more broadly) who are engaged in healing and self affirmation of who we are in the way that we are as a foundational task in the processes of research and teaching. This is a very productive space and I am looking forward to being in it with you.

---

2   This is a letter written to the African ascendant women in the Sisters of the Yam group that formed out of a necessity to affirm and understand the place of African cultural and spiritual identities within the context of our work in the academy. The names used here are pseudonyms for the members of the group.

THE POWER OF RITUALS AND TRADITIONS

I'm struck today by your comment, Yvonne, your deep concern and fearfulness about the level of honesty we can really bring to our space and time together here in the academy. My heart just broke (in recognition, mostly) as you so clearly articulated the "norm" in the academy and in society of being silenced, ignored, and shut down in our attempts to name and speak truth to racial issues, racial and cultural understandings, and to the racism we've experienced as Black women. And I was reminded of Audre Lorde's words about the transformation of silence into language and action. It's a quote I have hung over my computer, about the need for Black people to speak, regardless of the attempts by others to silence us. She says: "I was going to die, if not sooner then later, whether or not I had ever spoken myself. My silences had not protected me. Your silences will not protect you either" (Lorde, 1984, p. 41). She goes on to say what I believe is the real work needed to respond to being oppressed by others as we articulate our realities:

> But for every real word spoken, for every attempt I had ever made to speak those truths for which I am still seeking, I had made contact with other women, while we examined the words to fit a world in which we all believed, bridging our differences. And it was the concern and caring of all those women which gave me strength and enabled me to scrutinize the essentials of my living. (p. 41)

Speak. Speak. And speak some more. Speak until the words feel comfortable in your mouth. Speak them in ways that have love at the center, especially love of yourself. And speak them because we have the responsibility, once we have learned or healed ourselves, to go and teach, to heal someone else. And we heal and "fight the fight" as Yvonne suggested yesterday by showing up. Healthy. Strong. *Whole*. Embodying a keen sense of what OUR part of the work is, our *nia* (purpose) for being here at this moment on this earth in these bodies. And what beautiful bodies we are! Again Audre Lorde's (1984) words ring with truth here:

> My fullest concentration of energy is available to me only when I integrate all the parts of who I am, openly, allowing power from my particular sources of my living to flow back and forth freely through all my different selves, without the restriction of externally imposed definitions. Only then can I bring myself and my energies as a whole to the service of those struggles which I embrace as part of my living. (pp. 120–121)

I was struck by Sandra's strong conviction to live an honest life, to avoid lying or holding back. "I can't live like that," was her refrain. For me, that is the consciousness that we must consistently and always strive to express and live through, especially in an academic life. India.Arie's voice just popped in my head:

> And *I choose*, to be the best that I can be:
> I choose,
> to be courageous in everything I do.
> The path don't dictate who I am:
> I choose. (Arie, 2006)

Despite the anger. Despite the pain. Despite our weariness at folks continuing to expect us to teach them about race. Despite the ignorant questions and assumptions about African ascendant women. Debra's right: There are consequences for refusing to carry the burden of work that other people have not done and need to do for themselves. But each of us will need to answer some fundamental questions for ourselves. And as Chineze suggested, answering them is often by necessity solo work, work that we must first do in the quiet of our own spirits and souls:

- What is my work in the world, as an African ascendant woman?
- How do I manifest the work that is only mine to do?
- Who are the people who can help me to do my work?
- How do I stay committed and focused in the work and not get distracted or seduced by other peoples' work *for* me?
- Who am I working on behalf of? How will they (said community) know? Can they see this work in my everyday interactions and life?
- How do I "be" consistently myself, staying true to higher spiritual principles and powers, to something bigger than myself?

Kubosa raised the issue of shaming and how the missionary mentality is so deeply a part of the way Black women are regarded in U.S. society. How do we respond to that everyday assault on our spirits? My experiences suggest to me that part of our healing is wrapped up in our being honest and keeping a razor-sharp focus in dogged pursuit of our work. And I also believe a cohesive worldwide Black collective agenda requires us to be "individually" strong and healthy, body, mind, and spirit. So it is not a time to be trifling. It is the time to stop telling lies to ourselves about what we coulda/shoulda/woulda done or accomplished if not for (sexism, my awful ex-husband, a racist professor, a hurtful interaction with another sister, fill in the blank_____).

This is our life, the real show and not a dress rehearsal.

And Black people were created to call and recall, seen vividly in our tradition of call and response. And often the call arises from the voice of Spirit as we sit quietly with ourselves. As hooks (1993) suggests:

> Solitude is essential to the spiritual for it is there that we cannot only commune with divine spirits but also listen to our inner voice…without knowing how to be alone, we cannot know how to be with others and sustain the necessary autonomy. (p. 186)

As we contemplate the ways that anger and intimacy have influenced and continue to influence our lives and work as African ascendant women, I hope you will join me in spirit, sitting in quiet sometime this week, because we have mighty work to do. Light a candle. Chant. Pray. Be still and *know*. But mostly? Be peace.

Lesson #3: (Re)membering our beads provides us the strength, courage and wisdom to withstand the seductions that do not value who we are and the dignity to affirm ourselves, our memories, and our cultural knowledge and legacies.

Sankofa, Our Redemption Song, seen on the back cover of this book, is a prayer to the ancestors: Those who endured the cruel experiences of being captured and enslaved in Africa, survived the horrors of the Middle Passage, withstood the brutalities of slavery, endured the state-sponsored terrorism of lynching and massacre on these shores, and have lived and continue to live through the indignities that have been the experiences of being Black in America and elsewhere. And as an ascendant of African people, these experiences run through my blood and the blood of every person of African ascent in the diaspora, as well as on the continent of Africa today. This is our legacy, the gift that the ancestors gave to us. And in the words of the Akan people of Ghana, it is our duty to *san ko fa*: To return and fetch what we need of the strength, courage and wisdom of these ancestors and bring it forward to address the challenges of our lives in these times. *Sankofa is our redemption song*.

Turquoise and red beads, designed by my sister-friend Edna in the Krobos tradition of beadmaking in Ghana, anchor this strand. There are a total of 8 groups of 5 anchor beads or 40 anchor beads. This is a very spiritually significant number, especially in the Christian tradition. It is also said to be the number of days that it takes, once a commitment or goal is made, for that commitment to truly become a part of you, to embrace the strength and courage to work through new experiences and to change old ones that no longer serve your highest purpose. Powerful transformations can and do happen in 40 days. I often use this number in prayer beads, as it is an important reminder of the sort of commitment that it takes to embrace the difficult changes that come suddenly to our lives. Such was the case of our ancestors who were torn from their lands and families in Africa and whose blood was shed in that brutality. In the miles and miles that our ancestors walked through the bush in shackles. Of those who died in the slave dungeons along the west coast of Africa. Of the blood shed of the Middle Passage from disease, insurrections, and attack. Of that also shed in the New World on plantations, from the ends of lynching ropes, in civil rights movements, in governmental experiments. Such horror is hard to fathom. On the shawl, it is represented by 4 pairs of new and old "blood" beads. The old dark glass beads from Ghana are the blood of the families and loved ones who have witnessed and experienced our trials as Black people. Here, it is also important to recognize that the continent of Africa suffered the loss of her children and is still suffering those losses today. New red glass beads (India) represent the new blood of African people that is always influenced by the old: There *is* no African American without the African. And in addition to creating what we know as an African diaspora, this migration and mixing (often forced through rape, and after slavery, in our partnering with peoples of different ethnicities and cultural heritages) created a new Black people in the Western world: The Afro-Canadian, the African American, the Afro-Cuban, etc. These New World Africans are represented by the 12 black/white/and red layered beads, symbolizing our complexities and layeredness, often imperfect but always attached to Africa by both blood and Blackness. And I choose a dozen in reference also to "the dozens," one of the many manifestations of African understandings transformed and brought forward in the New World. We can point to other transformations, echoes of the voices of the ancestors: Jazz, gumbo, African American vernacular English, braiding and other hairstyles. *Sankofa* is always in us. Whether we are conscious of ourselves as connected to Africa or not, we engage in "going back to fetch" African understandings and ways of being as often as we take a breath.

African people have always had an important relationship with the natural world, that is, with the earth, sea, sky, sun, mountains, animals of the forest. And understanding the wisdom of those relationships, from an African standpoint, is part of *sankofa*. Four bright turquoise glass beads from India represent the sea and our understanding of the living spirit of the sea: It gives and supports life, and in the case of many of our ancestors who perished in the Middle Passage, provides the watery grave of their final resting place. And bones and shells are a strong part of *Sankofa, Our Redemption Song*. There are 3 fish bones. There is a cowry shell (or *cedie* in Twi) that I picked up on the sea shore in Ghana. The modern currency in Ghana is named *cedi*, as the cowry was used as currency in ancient times. These shells are also used as offerings to spirits when one desires the energy of the sea. Another seashell from the

Ghana shores, one that resembles a bone, is also a part of the strand. I love this shell, as it is through its difficult tumblings, a result of being pulled and tugged along the ocean bottom, that it became beautiful. This is the story of Black people everywhere! Finally there are two batiked bone beads made in Kenya. The large round one represents the continent of Africa. The smaller one represents the idea of Pan-Africanism and the attempts by at least some of our people and leaders to recognize the importance of *sankofa*. When you look carefully at this bead, you'll see the Ghanaian Adinkra symbol, Gye Nyame, meaning "One God." The full circle nature of Pan-Africanism is clear through this bead: A bead made in Kenya, East Africa, that bears witness to a language system and culture in Ghana, West Africa, that I bought in a store in Columbus, Ohio, in the United States of America and that will now travel to wherever the wearer of this shawl is going.

There are 8 turquoise glass beads from Ghana which represent the sky. I believe (and stories have told us) that it was through our ancestors' connections to God's creations (the sea, stars, sun, sky, etc.) that they were able to keep their faith: In the Creator, in spirit, in each other, in humanity, in connections to home that had been broken. One bright gold bead represents the sun. It is placed at the center back of the strand. And while it may often be "covered" by a collar or by someone's hair, it is still always present. These are the lessons that carried the ancestors through their trials and tribulations and from which we can draw inspiration and hope today.

Finally there are healing stones on this piece. I believe that engaging in our own versions of *sankofa* can be healing practices for Africans in diaspora. Silver is a feminine metal, very useful for introspection, reflection, and (re)membering. And "we are the daughters of those women who chose to survive," as Julie Dash says in her landmark film *Daughters of the Dust* (1991). There is a sterling silver ankh representing life and womanhood. It is in honor of the mothers and sisters of who have perished in the New World, in Africa, and in various versions of continued oppressions of Black women all over the globe. There is also one lone African trade bead on this strand. While not listed in any book on gemstones and metals, these trade beads are healing as they find their way to prayer work. Having been used as trading pieces for goods and later traded for African people in the transatlantic slave trade, I feel particularly healed to recover these beads that carry the cries and voices of the ancestors and to (re)member them in the work of collecting our beads. There is a lava stone bead and an orthoceras fossil, reminders of the ancient nature of wisdom. There are 2 faceted quartz beads, used to heal and align the spiritual and emotional body. These beads also remind me of the sparkle of the sea, something that always heals, when time allows me to spend hours and hours in its gaze. There are 3 clear Ghana glass beads, reminding us of the way that our ancestors recognized the energy of spirit in *everything*, including what we see today as inanimate objects. There is one large agate crystal rock bead, the "God" bead of the strand. This bead is also placed near the heart: That is where the ancestors must have carried their faith in Spirit, given the traumas they were going through. It is also where African people must place our faith today.

Agates are often used for clearing and grounding. The 3-hole red agate at the bottom of *Sankofa, Our Redemption Song* can be used to calm and stabilize emotions. We must (re)member our purposes and be about the work of fulfilling them! The spotted agate disc on the other side of the strand is used to cleanse and clear our auras. It can act as a magnet for negative energy, cleansing and transforming that negative energy into something positive. It reminds us that the ancestors' voices whisper to us often: "Sankofa is your redemption song." And so it is.

Lesson #4: (Re)membering our beads encourages us to see ourselves spiritually, as being in the world but not of it, and always on purpose.

Awakening in Africa: A Meditation[3]

I woke up today
In Africa,
And it wasn't simply
The act of opening my eyes
And stretching my body after a long rest
I actually "woke up" in Africa!
Realizing not
The absence of sleep
But the presence of being
Fully alive
In Africa!

Sometimes as an ascendant
Of this great continent
Whose life has mostly
Been lived in North America,
It is easy to fall asleep
To that which is essentially
African inside...
But in Your gift of my being here, Creator,
You've awakened me to

---

[3] "Awakening in Africa" is a meditation from my unpublished manuscript entitled *Living Africa: A Book of Meditations*.

My African self,
The very essence of me.
Yes, my soul woke up in Africa!
And while I hardly realized
How deeply my spirit yearned for this awakening
All of the days of my life,
I now realize
Just how powerful I am when
All of me—
Mind, body and spirit
Are awake in Africa!

I opened my eyes today.
And I was in Africa!
Way down deep
In Africa!
And I will never fall asleep again!
Instead, I will only rest
In the peacefulness
Of my African soul
Still.
Rich.
Full of life
    Love
    Breath
    And wonder
In Africa!
Thank you God!

A (not so) final note: A place for ritual in teaching and research

> "How dare he boast of victory," [the lioness] complains,
> "when neither of us won the battle?"
> "No one challenges the hunter," returns a wizened old headwoman…
> *"until the lioness learns to tell her own story."*
> (Jackson-Opoku, 1997, p. 11, emphasis mine)

(Re)membering rituals and traditions is no small task. Collecting our beads, the legacy of stories and the cultural and spiritual activities handed down from generation to generation, often also involves collecting what has been passed on orally, from relatives seen and ancestors unseen. But here is the key: Rituals, like beads, are creative: They can be brought to bear in/on any activity by virtue of active and sincere gratitude for and recognition of the legacy of wisdom and ways of being of African people, both in the diaspora and on the continent of Africa. As such, the teacher and researcher is being asked here to recognize the layers of memories that are forever present to us, waiting to be strung together, honored and appreciated as the precious and beautiful beads that they are. And for African ascendant persons, they are a part and parcel of the spiritual lessons necessary to (re)member our personhood, our histories, our cultural knowledge, our inheritance. As mentioned, while rituals from an endarkened feminist perspective arise from a space of memory, they are also cultural, spiritual, and social in origin and purpose. They are embedded in the small and grand practices of (re)membering, acts that keep the whole community of the living and the dead united, the forces of life in harmony from season to season. I am suggesting here that rituals become rituals when the ancestors are *regularly* (re)membered for their continuing protection and thanked for the wise and beautiful legacy they left behind. But for these (re)memberings to be rituals, we also must *do* something. (Re)membering traditions and engaging rituals arise from the raw material—the wise beads—that are available to us, as we tell our stories and gather those rolling around us, stringing them together in new and beautiful ways. In each of the memories above, we see that memory and connections across waters and boundaries of generation, time, and space are sought and explored, ending in a deeper recognition of the sacred nature of everyday existence, one that is life affirming for the African ascendant in diaspora and lived in honor of the inheritance of the ancestors and the legacy of which we are a part as African ascendant people.

Hence, there is a need in our teaching and research to recognize and understand the deeper meanings of rituals and spiritual knowledges in our educational contexts and in our ways of engaging inquiry. This is a kind of teaching that truly honors the complexities we so often experience in our bodies, minds, and spirits. A kind of teaching that is both dialogical and multiple, both spiritual and sacred. A kind of teaching that is both historical and cultural, that honors the fluidity of time and space, of the material world and the spiritual one. Mostly, we need a kind of teaching and research that acknowledges both the joy and pain of location, dislocation, and the rituals that may help us to transform both in our memories and in the present. African women are not stories of a singular self but are stories of *we*: That we-ness is often manifest in rituals deeply embedded in African women's wisdom and knowledge, our strands of wisdom.

What rituals can we see in our acts of teaching and research, beads that affirm African ascendant women, both generally and specifically? What are the deeper meanings of the rituals we ourselves engage in and how do we share the cultural memories that undergird them? How do we hear and imagine the depth of meaning of African ascendant ritual and tradition without trying to make them into something that can only be compared to that of another? What do the diverse stories of African memory mean to us and what emotions and memories do they evoke in us? How do our own memories and emotions mediate, extend, or distort those of others? These are the questions we might consider in bringing ritual and tradition to bear in teaching and research. For it is when we can bring awareness (the worth of who African people are, have been, and what we know), vigilance (the need to safeguard African knowledge and rituals), strength (the will and ability to resist being seduced away from our cultural and spiritual inheritance as Africans) and a stance both on and in the world that honors spiritual wealth through material being and conditions (Marshall, 1984), that we will have strands of beads worthy to wear and a celebratory space worthy of them.

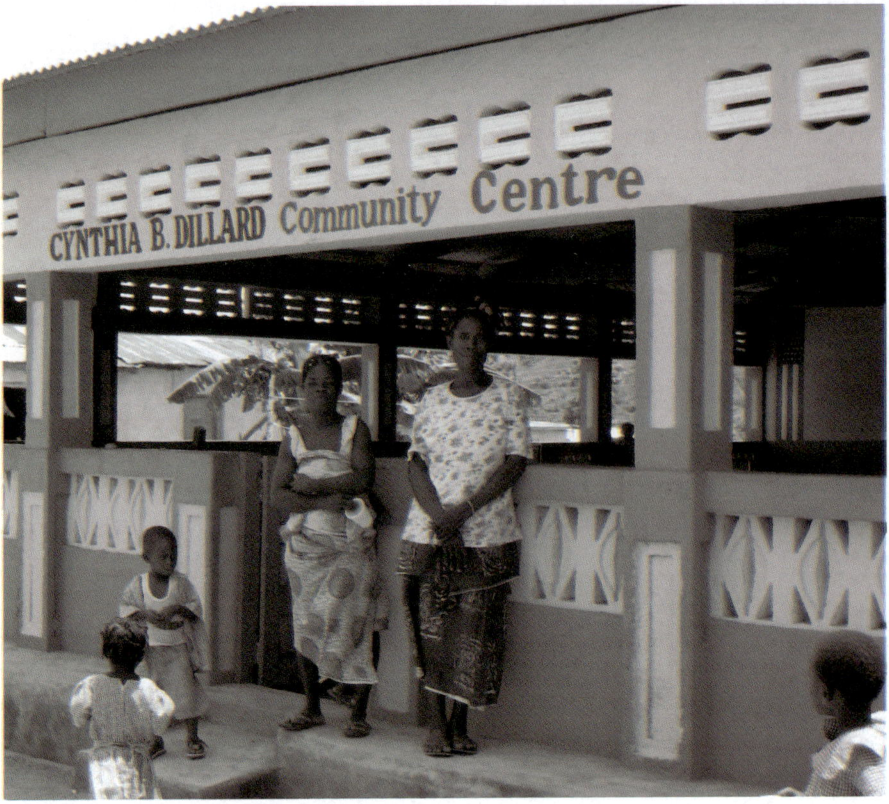
CYNTHIA B. DILLARD Community Centre

CHAPTER FIVE

The Importance of Naming

Spirituality, the Sacred, and New Questions for Endarkened Transnational Feminist Research

WITH CHINWE OKPALAOKA

I.
Sankofa Means Go Back to Fetch It: Revisiting Paradigms[1]

> History is sacred because it is the only chance that you have of knowing who you are outside of what's been rained down upon you from a hostile environment. And when you go to the documents created inside the culture, you get another story. You get another history. The history is sacred and the highest, most hallowed songs in tones are pulled into service to deliver that story (Latta, 1992).

Several years ago, responding to Scheurich and Young's (1997) *Educational Researcher* article "Coloring Epistemologies: Are Our Research Epistemologies Racially Biased?" a number of researchers presented sessions at national meetings, wrote papers, and responded to the challenge inherent in Scheurich and Young's rather provocative title.[2] Among other writings, my modest contribution to this paradigm talk became a chapter in my first book (Dillard, 2006a). There, I explored the cultural, political, and spiritual nature of the entire conversation about paradigms and the way that the swirling assumptions and conclusions about their proliferation were mostly carried

---

1   In honor of the long traditions of proverbs in the African and African diasporic communities, we introduce each section of this chapter with an Adinkra proverb that represents the focus of the section. For further reading on the language of Adinkra symbols, see Willis (1998).

2   "Coloring epistemologies" was a descriptive termed used by Scheurich and Young (1997) of the ways that traditional research epistemologies were being created, centered with/in identity markers such as race, culture, class, gender, national origin, religion, and marshaled in research projects, primarily by people of color. Tyson's response in *Educational Researcher* (1998) critiques this notion on the basis of its unexamined assumptions and implicit racist implications. The idea of "paradigm proliferation" was an extension of the same argument, that is, that paradigms represented what is known and upheld as legitimizing knowledge in research. Thus, the discussion of proliferation of paradigms (again, particularly given that they are being advanced by people of color) continued to also advance the same racist assumptions. See Dillard (2006b) for an examination and critique of the paradigm proliferation.

out at a level of abstraction (and distraction), absent any examination of the ways that racism, power, and politics profoundly shape our research and representations, especially as scholars of color. I spoke to how such exclusion "brings a particularized paradox for scholars of color as we seek to imagine, create and embrace new and useful paradigms from and through which we engage educational research…[as] there are deep and serious implications in choosing to embrace paradigms that resonate with our spirit as well as our intellect, regardless of issues of 'proliferation'" (Dillard, 2006a, pp. 29–30). I raised up the all too common absence of Black voices and voices of scholars of color in the discussions of the meanings and outcomes of the "coloring" of epistemologies, a discussion that had been carried out as if we did not exist as subjects within the conversation but solely as objects of it, invisible and silent. However well intentioned, Black people and our thoughts about paradigms were the focus of the steady and often distorted gaze and descriptions of White researchers.

The part of the discussion that still resonates with me most deeply today (and with many students of qualitative research) is the call for scholars of color to turn our attention and desires away from "belonging" to a particular paradigm (or even to the discussion of paradigm proliferation that still often swirls around us *but does not include us*), and instead to construct and nurture paradigms that encompass and embody our cultural and spiritual understandings, memories, and the histories that shape our epistemologies and ways of being.

We see evidence of the same call echoed throughout the literature on qualitative research. Ladson-Billings' (2000) contrasts the concept of individualism and the elevation of the individual mind prevalent in Western thought, with the African notion of *Ubuntu* ("I am because we are"), explored in more depth in Chapter 6. The notion of individual well-being that is predicated on the wholeness of the community speaks to the same spiritual and epistemological stance of endarkened feminist epistemology. Ladson-Billings' reference to the necessity of using different discourses and epistemologies that can disrupt Western epistemological discourse/the dominant worldview can be interpreted as an echo of an endarkened transnational feminism, whose notions of the sacred and the spiritual in research disrupts the Western tendency to bifurcate the mind and the spirit. Further, she suggests that we must research and better understand "well developed systems of knowledge…that stand in contrast to the dominant Euro-American epistemology" (p. 258) in order to address the critical questions of the world today. This is part of a larger effort by scholars of color and of conscience to address the ravages of racism and other discriminations and to create a space of freedom for all humanity. Hence, our exploration of endarkened and transnational feminisms here is an extension of the same need that encouraged an entire volume on critical and indigenous methodologies (Denzin, Lincoln, & Tuhiwai-Smith,

2008). Central to this volume is the embrace of indigenous and critical research epistemologies which foreground spirituality including feminist, Native, indigenous, endarkened and Black feminist, spiritual, hybrid, Chicana, and border/Mestizaje among others. We also see in these works gestures towards a more sacred nature of science, an idea that Reason (1993) forwarded more than a decade ago. In this work, his call is for researchers to consider how spirituality and the sacred can be brought to bear on pressing human and environmental problems. Our chapter here is a response to Reason's call. Our attempt is to both examine the complexities of Black and endarkened feminisms and epistemologies that link the continent of Africa and the African diaspora, bringing discourses of the spiritual and the sacred to bear in this discussion in a way that is fundamentally about naming. It is also recognition of a needed discussion still missing in the literature of multiple epistemologies and theories of research.

With the publication of *On Spiritual Strivings* (2006a) and the global reaction to it, I found myself (and my students) wondering more deeply about the way that knowledge travels and moves in the world, enlarging and engaging the discussions and constructions of what it means to be a Black woman and particularly, what it will mean for those who are Black women scholars. As the work continued to travel, new opportunities for dialogue and cooperation also arose, including with the co-author of this chapter, Chinwe Okpalaoka, who ascends from Nigeria. In our conversations as sister-scholars, we began to recognize not just the spiritual but the *sacred* nature of research that African ascendant women have always done and are continuing to do all over the globe. We believe it is the same sacred and divine energy that has brought us together to do this writing.

Some definitions of key terms may be important here. An *endarkened feminist epistemology* (Dillard, 2000, 2006b) articulates how reality is known when based in the historical roots of global Black feminist thought. More specifically, such an epistemology embodies a distinguishable difference in cultural standpoint from mainstream (White) feminism in that it is located in the intersection/overlap of the culturally constructed notions of race, gender, class, national, and other identities. Maybe most importantly, it arises from and informs the historical and contemporary contexts of oppressions and resistance for African ascendant women. From an endarkened feminist epistemological space, we are encouraged to move away from the traditional metaphor of research as recipe to fix a "problem" to a metaphor that centers in/on reciprocity and relationship between the researcher and the researched, between knowing, the production of knowledge, and its use. Thus, I have forwarded the idea that a more useful research metaphor of research from an endarkened feminist epistemological stance is research as a responsibility, answerable and obligated to the very persons and communities being engaged in the inquiry (Dillard, 2000, 2006b).

Our use of the term "transnational" is a literal one. We are simply meaning a way of engaging endarkened feminism that is beyond or through (*trans*) the boundaries of nations. But we also believe that such engagements bring to bear the possibility of a change in our worldsense (Oyewumi, 2005) as well.

An endarkened feminist epistemology is also an approach to research that honors the wisdom, memory, spirituality, and critical interventions of transnational Black woman's ways of knowing and being in research, with the sacred serving as a way to describe the doing of it, the way that we approach the work. Noting the distinction between spirituality and the sacred is important here. What we mean by *spirituality* is to have a consciousness of the realm of the spirit in one's work and to recognize that consciousness as a transformative force in research and teaching (Alexander, 2005; Moraga & Anzaldúa, 1981; Dillard, 2006a, 2006b; Dillard, Tyson, & Abdur-Rashid 2000; Fernandes, 2003; hooks, 1994; Hull, 2001; Ryan, 2005; Wade-Gayles, 1995). However, when we speak of the *sacred* in endarkened feminist research, we are referring to the way the work is honored and embraced as it is carried out. Said another way, work that is sacred is worthy of being held with reverence as it is done. The idea here is that, as we consider paradigms and epistemology from endarkened or Black feminist positions, the work embodies and engages spirituality and is carried out in sacred ways. Thus, we are using the notions of both spirituality and sacredness to explore more globally the meanings, articulations, and possibilities of an endarkened feminist epistemology and research as sacred, spiritual, and relevant practices of inquiry for Black women on the continent of Africa and throughout her diaspora. Mostly, we are suggesting that both spirituality and the sacred are embedded fundamentally in the very ground of inquiry, knowledge, and cultural production of Black women's lives and experiences and that it is this understanding that helps us to understand the radical activism of Black feminism transnationally. However, as we look back to the earlier articulations of the cultural and spiritual nature and work of paradigms for scholars of color, what is missing is an explicit attention to the epistemologies of Black or endarkened feminism in an interconnected, intersubjective, and transnational way that renders visible the work of research as sacred work, centered in the spiritual notions constructed by Black women on the continent and in the diaspora.

Whether in the U.S., Africa, or in the African diaspora, women of African ascent share experiences with some form of oppression characterized and related by our class, race, or gender, by our existence as women. And often, it is some version of or belief in spirit that has allowed us to stand in the face of hostility and degradation, however severe (Akyeampong & Obeng, 2005; Alexander, 2005; Dillard, 2006a, 2006b; hooks, 1994; Hull, 2001; Keating, 2008; Moraga & Anzaldúa, 1981; Walker,

2006). Most arguments that have arisen around similarities and differences in transnational Black women's experience with interlocking oppressions have focused on whether there exists a hierarchy of oppressions for women on the African continent versus in the African diaspora and the issue of appropriate naming of the struggle (Hudson-Weems, 1998b; Walker, 1983; Nnaemeka, 1998; Steady, 1981). This is a discussion we take up later in this chapter.

However, such ground leads us to several questions that guide our examination here. What are the contours of Black or endarkened feminist epistemology and paradigms that emerge from African women's voices and spirits *transnationally*? What are the tensions, the cultural and historical experiences, diversities, nuances, and relationships that have created visions and versions of Black women's thinking, theorizing, and praxis that in/exclude Black feminism, Africana womanism, and other theoretical frameworks for Black women's thinking and being with/against one another? Where is memory and spirituality in these global discussions and how do they matter to the work of research? To its methods, methodologies, and representations? Most importantly, we seek to further explore the profound question—and the equally profound response—put forth by M. Jacqui Alexander in her groundbreaking work *Pedagogies of Crossing: Meditations on Feminism, Sexual Politics, Memory, and the Sacred* (2005):

> What would taking the Sacred seriously mean for transnational feminism and related radical projects beyond an institutionalized use value of theorizing marginalization? *It would mean wrestling with the praxis of the Sacred.* (p. 326, emphasis ours)

It means exploring and creating sacred versions and approaches to research and a critical revisioning of the very meanings of Black feminist inquiry and paradigms. It means taking up spirituality and the sacred as a place "from which to launch a critique of the status quo" (Wright, 2003, p. 209) from a Black-eyed female gaze. It means (re)membering what others have hoped we'd forgotten.

II.

Nyame Nti (Since God exists): Exploring the cultural and historical landscape of Endarkened/Black feminist perspectives of research in Africa and the Diaspora

> Everything we engage in our lives is primarily a practice ordered by spirit, or authorized by spirit and executed by someone who recognizes that [she] cannot, by herself, make happen what she has been invited towards. (Some, 1994)

According to Nnaemeka (1998), discussions about the condition of African world women on the continent and in the diaspora must by necessity center around "common ground while respecting the nuances that make the emergence of a monolith impossible" (Nnaemeka, 1998, p. 3). We extend this notion of commonality, or what Collins (2000) calls "a common agenda" (p. 237), by focusing, at the end of this chapter, on the common themes of struggle and spirituality shared through Black feminisms within Africa, the U.S. and the diaspora, as well as epistemological and methodological questions we might consider that speak to this agenda. By doing this we acknowledge both the depth of cultural memories and "the power of sisterhood" (Nnaemeka, 1998, p. 4), even within the variances of oppressions and experiences of Black women worldwide.

The concepts of intersecting oppressions and domination, though universal in practice, take on varying forms of expression from one society to another (Collins, 2000). Collins suggests that the shape of domination changes as it takes on specific forms across temporal, historical and geographical contexts. The key difference lies in the organization of particular oppressions. Said another way, though contexts of domination might be similar across the globe (in that there is some combination of interlocking systems of oppression), the differences arise in the ways these particular oppressions manifest and the historical roots of said oppressions. The type of clothing that oppression is dressed in (that is, apartheid, colonialism, imperialism, enslavement) may vary. However, they are all systems of oppression, intersecting in various combinations and contexts. Ultimately, Collins' (2000) suggests that it is fundamentally about whose knowledge and methodology is front, center, and definitive. In order to think about and work through the differences across the continent and diaspora, we must find that "common agenda."

Collins (2000) was not alone in her clarion call for a transnational Black feminism to confront intersecting oppressions of race, class, gender, and sexuality across the globe. She was joined by many including Obioma Nnaemeka, a groundbreaking Black feminist scholar from Nigeria. Yet, a closer look at the historical and sociological manifestations of oppression and domination of endarkened or Black feminist thought in the African diaspora reveals a sort of dynamism, a constantly changing nature of oppressions for African ascendant women, very particular within and across national contexts. For example, although interlocking oppressions of race, class, gender, and sexuality characterize Black women's experiences in the African diaspora, the particular oppression that dominates might differ from one geographical and national context to another. Nnaemeka (1998) speaks of multiple feminisms within the countries of Africa and even between Africa and other continents as an indication of multiplicity of perspectives. She further explains that the multiplicity of perspectives must include cultural and historical forces that have fueled women's movements in Africa. Nnaemeka describes the African feminist spirit as both "complex and diffused" (p. 5):

> The much bandied-about intersection of class, race, sexual orientation, etc., in Western feminist discourse does not ring with the same urgency for most African women, for whom other basic issues of everyday life are intersecting in most oppressive ways. This is not to say that issues of race and class are not important to African women in the continent....African women see and address such issues first as they configure in and relate to their own lives and immediate surroundings. (p. 7)

Collins (2000) urges us to think globally when we consider the shared legacy of struggle and oppressions and (re)member that the experiences of women of African ascent have been shaped by varying forms of domination including slavery and colonialism. The oppression of continental African women cannot be isolated from the persistent consequences of colonialism. In other words, as Nnaemeka (1998) frames it, "to meaningfully explain...African feminism, it is... to the African environment that one must refer..." (p. 9). Likewise, the oppressions of African ascendant women in the diaspora cannot be isolated from the persistent consequences of centuries of enslavement. It is noteworthy that the 1960s were turbulent times for African ascendant people on the continent in the fight for independence from colonial rule and those in the diaspora engaged in various Civil Rights movements. While the former fought to gain independence from colonial rulers, the latter marched for the rights of Black Americans, women, the disabled, and other marginalized groups.

A historical survey of the roots of Black feminism in the U.S. and on the continent of Africa may help situate Black women's experiences with oppression on the globe, the ground from which interventions and transformations of research must arise. Although we begin this discussion with a brief history of Black feminism, we do not believe that U.S. Black feminism marked the beginning of feminism for women of color all over the world. In fact, there are on-going critiques of U.S (and European) Black feminisms and the dangers of the cultural hegemony throughout the world, particularly from continental African feminist scholars. U.S. Black feminism continues to play an important role in global discussions on Black women's experiences with oppression. While the holistic nature of interlocking systems of oppression has not been particular to U.S. Black feminists, it has provided the stage for reconceptualizing and (re)membering new relationships within and between African women's spirits and experiences in the diaspora and the African continent and shaping research paradigms and methodology as well. Black feminists in the United States context may have strong understandings of experiences and struggles as African ascendant women in the U.S., but too often there is precious little understanding or knowledge of the experiences and struggles of African ascendant women throughout the rest of the diaspora and on the continent of Africa. This is our attempt to bring our herstories to bear across the globe in a way that allow us to create paradigms across our differences "that resonate with our spirit as well as our intellect, regardless of issues of proliferation" (Dillard, 2006b, pp. 29–30). These are paradigms of memory.

U.S. Black feminism in brief (by Cynthia Dillard)

I remember being very powerfully influenced by the image of Angela Davis in the 1970s. And it wasn't simply the perfect Afro that framed her face like a crown that moved me: It was the powerful sound of her voice as she talked about freedom and truth and Black women's struggles in the United States and beyond. I remember my own desires to be a part of the Black Panther Party, but I wasn't quite of age. However, when I saw those brothers (and an occasional sister) walking into my former elementary school to serve lunches to children who needed them most, that act was transformational for me. I realized in that moment that whatever "Black Power" meant, it included the commitment to knowing our history, enacting our culture with spirit, and engaging in social and sacred action on behalf of Black people, especially the young and those most needy.

While my parents were involved with more mainstream Black organizations (the Links and Omega Psi Phi), I was more interested in what were deemed the more "radical" Black organizations. And I was especially interested in the places where Black *women* were organizing, marching, making their voices heard. The National Black Feminist Organization (NBFO) was one of the first Black feminist organizations with an explicit commitment to confronting the interlocking systems of racism, sexism, and heterosexism that plagued Black women in the United States. Emerging in 1973, the organization was also a forceful response to the lack of attention and regard for Black women's experiences within both the women's movement and within Black power movements witnessed above (Wallace, 1982; Hull, Bell-Scott, & Smith, 1982). By 1974, a spin-off group of U.S. Black feminists formed the Combahee River Collective, focusing on a more radical commitment to fight the oppressions that Black women still faced in the United States. The mission of this group of women, in comparison to the NBFO, was to confront these complex systems of oppression through a Black feminist political movement (Combahee River Collective, 1982). Rather than project themselves as "firsts" or as pioneers of Black feminism, the collective's members acknowledged their work as an extension of the earlier work of Black women activists like Sojourner Truth, Harriet Tubman, Frances E.W. Harper, Ida B. Wells Barnett, and Mary Church Terrell, whose intellectual and activist work flourished during the post-slavery era (Combahee River Collective, 1982). There was also a very strong commitment to *spiritually* center the work of the Combahee River Collective, both in the sacred approach to seeing and acknowledging the foundational role of Black women ancestors and in setting a purpose and vision that sought to transform the social and political milieu away from oppression and toward equality and justice, particularly for U.S. Black women.

By the early 1970s, we witnessed a critical intervention of Black women's theorizing and knowledge production, as Black feminist literature (including anthologies and fiction) began to be published and find their way to bookstores and bookshelves, both in the U.S. and abroad. This was not simply publishing as an economic intervention in the lives and knowledges of Black women: This was a radical intervention, as these literatures fundamentally shifted and shaped the foundations of feminist thought generally and Black feminist thought and action in particular. Toni Cade Bambara's *The Black Woman: An Anthology* (1970), Toni Morrison's *The Bluest Eye* (1970), Audre Lorde's *Cables to Rage* (1970), Alice Walker's *In Search of Our Mothers' Gardens: Womanist Prose* (1983), and a reissue of Zora Neale Hurston's *Their Eyes Were Watching God* (1978) are examples of landmark literary texts that defined and theorized the early Black feminist movement in the United States. As an African American adolescent girl, I felt these early works profoundly as I sought desperately to define what it meant to be both Black and female in the predominately White schooling contexts of my youth. All of the texts we were required to read centered images of White womanhood as virtuous and worthy of emulation. Louisa May Alcott's *Little Women* was the standard to which we were asked to aspire, and watching *The Brady Bunch* was the free time entertainment of the day. But my mother's version of Black womanhood (albeit similarly tethered to homemaking and child rearing as Mrs. Brady) was tied to a simple and explicit truth, manifest in her strict attention to our school lives, homework, and consistent trips to the public library: Education and learning to read the word and the world were the *only* ways to create options for Black women's lives. In her precious free time, my mother read these texts along with me, opening me to a world that in some cases highlighted the harsh realities of her own life as a Black woman, growing up in poverty and during segregation in the United States. In other cases, these words on the page opened something that didn't simply exist only in my mother's imagination and my own but that also existed as *possibilities for us*. Further, these texts stirred significant debates and controversies within the Black community, especially for Black men, who often resented what they interpreted as direct accusations that they were perpetrators of gender and sexual oppression. Regardless of the consequences, my mom and I continued to read every story of Black womanhood we could. And I learned how powerful words could be: Black women's literature helped us define ourselves for ourselves, and as an oral tradition, it goes back generations. Now, through the voices of Walker, Hurston and others, as well as the words on the page, we could *see* our definitions and return to them over and over again.

The 1980s brought more radical overtly political texts, responding in part to the birth of woman's studies and specifically Black women's thought and knowledge production "in public." We came to know, through their writings, major Black feminist scholars who were also activists like Gloria (Akasha) Hull, Barbara Smith, and Patricia Bell-Scott, whose co-edited text (Hull, Bell-Scott, & Smith, 1982), *All the Women Are White, All the Blacks Are Men, but Some of Us Are Brave* became a pioneering text for Black feminist studies across the United States. This relative proliferation of Black feminist writing in the 1980s also included works like Barbara Smith's *Home Girls: A Black Feminist Anthology* (1983) and bell hooks's (1981) *Ain't I a Woman?: Black Women and Feminism,* which focused on the impact of sexism on Black women. But these women also began to bring questions and concerns of sexual identities and spirituality within Black feminism to the forefront. Lorde's *Sister Outsider* (1984) spoke directly to the need for integration and wholeness in Black women's multifaceted identities, including our sexualities. Paule Marshall's *Praisesong for the Widow* (1984) brought to the fore the ways that remembering culture and history as a Black woman is truly transformative, particularly from a spiritual perspective.

This Bridge Called My Back: Writings by Radical Women of Color (Moraga & Anzaldúa, 1981) was one of the earliest attempts to link the underlying oppressions of women across differences of race, class, sexuality, and culture. Equally important, Anzaldúa brought the scholarship and voices of women of color together in an edited volume that began to speak explicitly about the importance of spirituality, healing, and self-recovery as necessities for women of color across our ethnicities and identities.

The proliferation of scholarship of the 1990s and beyond picked up Anzaldúa's call to recognize the sacred and spiritual ethos of Black and endarkened feminisms. From hooks's (1993) *Sisters of the Yam: Black Women and Self-recovery* and Bambara's *The Salt Eaters* (1980/1992) to Collins's (1990) landmark, *Black Feminist Thought: Knowledge, Consciousness, and the Politics of Empowerment,* these texts literally transformed our understandings of gender, race, and class, centering them firmly in the epistemologies and theories of Black womanhood. It is interesting to note that one of the most radical revisions in Collins's second edition of *Black Feminist Thought* (2000) was her exploration of the limits of a Black feminism bounded by nationality: The revisions provided direction for how to place U.S. Black feminist thought into coalition with the voices and efforts of African ascendant women worldwide. And whether on the continent of Africa, in the United States, or all of the spaces between, around, and among them, we see that the creation of Black feminism in the United States is only a part of a living, breathing worldwide legacy of Black women. As Pearl Cleage (2005) suggests, Black/endarkened feminist thought is *itself* a praisesong:

> the flesh and blood of our collective dreaming,
> [through which] we realize with a knowing deeper than the flow of human blood in human veins
> that we are part of something *better, truer, deeper*. (p. 15)

At least part of the "better, truer, deeper" is found in the connections between Black feminism in the United States and efforts of African feminists on the continent, toward which we now turn.

Black feminism in Africa in brief (by Chinwe Okpalaoka)

While the struggle of U.S. Black feminists in the 1960s included the fight for the rights of women and people of color, Africans on the continent of Africa witnessed a decade that ushered in the end of colonial rule in many African nations. As former colonizers retreated to their countries of origin, newly formed African nations began what has been and continues to be an arduous and complicated journey toward independence. Oyeronke Oyewumi (1997) asserts that colonization should not be understood solely in the context of the period of the actual colonization. For many, she suggests, the period of the Atlantic slave trade and colonization "were logically one process unfolding over many centuries" (p. xi). This argument is critical to understanding the spiritual connection between African women on the continent and throughout the diaspora in our knowledge production and in praxis. And as Dillard (2006a) asserts, these connections are *always* present, whether we are conscious of them or not. It is an understanding and embrace of this connection that drew me to Dillard shortly after our first meeting. Soon after I began my doctoral studies, I was introduced to the histories of African Americans and theories about their lived experiences. As Oyewumi (1997) argues above, I quickly identified a connection between myself (as "representative" of the sister who never left the continent) and my African American sister ("representative" of those who were enslaved and taken from the continent of Africa). My dilemma, then, was how to gain legitimacy to speak on behalf of women from both sides of the Atlantic Ocean. Was I now estranged from my sister because I did not make that trip with her? Was I no longer a part of her story because we were now divided by history, distance, and experience? Did she not understand that I, too, knew the pain of oppression, albeit in a different form and intensity? That at the same time she was fighting for human rights in the United States, I was fighting to end centuries of oppression that began with slavery and continue today as neocolonialism? It is this connection of struggle and spirit that we speak in this chapter.

Amina Mama (2007) connects the advent of African independence struggles with the emergence of feminist activism in Africa, most notably in Nigeria and Egypt. However, many argue that gender, as a political category, was not necessarily a salient category for women in many African societies, especially in comparison to Black American feminists (Aina, 1998; Oyewumi, 1997; Taiwo, 2003). Although African nations were beginning the slow process of achieving independence from colonial regimes, women's issues were not foregrounded in this independence struggle. Continental African women quickly learned that the fight for independence did not necessarily place women's rights front and center in the fight for independence. Speaking specifically about Nigerian women, Molara Ogundipe-Leslie (1994) explains that the seeming lack of focus on women's issues post-independence could be explained by the preexistence and availability of economic opportunities for women in precolonial Nigeria. This is echoed by Ifi Amadiume (1987) in her precolonial, colonial, and post-independence analysis of the ways that women enjoyed relative power and influence, which diminished in eastern Nigeria only with the advent of British colonialism and its own versions of gender roles. This study counters the master narrative among Western feminists that portrays African women as having had limited political and economic power in comparison to their male counterparts. Amadiume demonstrates the way that colonialism actually disempowered women by limiting the economic freedom that they enjoyed in precolonial times. We see this echoed in prominent African feminist literature that theorizes women's lives, such as Kenyan Margaret Ogola's (2004) novel, *The River and the Source,* Nigerian Flora Nwapa's (1966) *Efuru,* and Ghanaian writer Ama Ata Aidoo's (1970) collection of short stories, entitled *No Sweetness Here and Other Stories.* Having spent the first 25 years of my life in eastern Nigeria, I witnessed, firsthand, the spirit of enterprise and economic independence that characterized women's efforts at running their households. Traditionally, men were the heads of households, but it was apparent that women were the glue that held the home front together. I understood, even as a young girl, why many women set up their own businesses, even when said business was a small table strategically placed in front of her home from which she hawked basic household and food items, while remaining within eyesight of her home and children. Although I wondered how much profit the women made from selling such small items, I understood that it was a powerful gesture toward economic independence and empowerment: A woman who depended entirely on her husband for financial help was usually perceived as lazy. So, the struggle for independence for the African woman was not necessarily a struggle for her economic independence but a struggle for the independence of her local and national community at large. Several scholars claim that the struggle for economic opportunities and the right to work, which characterized the struggles of women in the diaspora and elsewhere, could not easily be applied to women on the continent of Africa (Bray, 2008; Mohanty, Russo, & Torres, 1991; Nnaemeka, 1998; Ogundipe-Leslie, 1994). Instead, it was and continues to be neocolonialism, oppressive regimes, and marriage and cultural norms that we must unpack to understand the African woman's experience with oppression in Africa and her feminisms. Ama Ata Aidoo (1998) and Zulu Sofola (1998) concur that the African woman's burdens of oppression can be traced to both internal influences from sociocultural and patriarchal structures and external influences stemming from colonialism and postcolonial crises of leadership. Aidoo (1998) voices these sentiments when she states:

> Three major historical factors have influenced the position of the African woman today: Indigenous African social patterns; the conquest of the continent by Europe; and the apparent lack of vision, or courage, in the leadership of the post-colonial period. (p. 42)

Like her African ascendant sisters in the diaspora, the African woman on the continent of Africa has had to fight the voicelessness caused by centuries of domination through slavery, colonialism, and imperialism. She, too, has had to confront intersecting oppressions of racism, sexism, and classism. But the multiplicity of manifestations of the particular set of oppressions that plague women within and outside of the African continent has caused African feminists like Aidoo, Abena Busia, Sofola, Ogundipe-Leslie to advocate for the consideration of *culture* as a form of oppression for the African woman. According to Ogundipe-Leslie (1994) culture, much more than race, more aptly determines African women's identity. We understand that the three major axes of oppression (race, class, and gender), which may plague Black women in the diaspora (and within and against which we have theorized our versions of feminisms), must be expanded to include oppressive cultural norms. In this way, we may avoid thinking of African womanhood in universal terms, a tension that is apparent in many discussions of transnational Black feminisms (Collins, 2000; Guy-Sheftall, 1995; Ogundipe-Leslie, 1994; Omolade, 1994; Oyewumi, 1997; Steady, 1981). Nowhere is this wrestling more apparent than in the naming of what Nnaemeka (1998) calls the "feminist spirit" across the globe, to which we now turn.

Call me by my true names: Naming Black feminism in the United States, the Diaspora and the continent of Africa

Within African culture, naming is a sacred practice, one that is not only important to the continuation of the group's heritage and work but also to the purpose and future work of the individual being named. Through this issue of naming, we can begin to see the interconnected nature of Black feminist struggles in the United States with those of Black women throughout the diaspora and the continent of Africa.

Given the too often exclusionary spaces for U.S. Black feminists within the broader conversations of feminism, early Black feminists in the United States began to create names that more carefully honored and described a collective *Black* feminism. Walker (1983) first introduced the term *womanism* into the ongoing debates by White feminists, who seemed to quickly forget that their Black counterparts had been their allies nearly a decade before in the fight for civil rights. According to Walker, a womanist is

> a black feminist or feminist of color...a woman who loves other women, sexually and/or nonsexually...committed to survival and wholeness of entire people, male *and* female...Womanist is to feminist as purple is to lavender. (pp. xi–xii, emphasis hers)

However, in direct criticism of Walker's definition, Clenora Hudson-Weems (1998a, 1998b) argues that, regardless of where women of African heritage exist, we should not adopt the label of feminist because, in comparison to our Western counterparts, gender is not primary in the struggle for equity and recognition. Hudson-Weems (1995) prefers the term *Africana womanism* to womanism, Black feminism, and African feminism. She believes that Africana womanism more succinctly captures the family centeredness in an African framework, rather than the female centeredness of Western feminism. This also resonates with the stance that many continental African feminists have taken, suggesting the crucial need for African men and women to come together to confront all oppression, given what is seen as the interdependency of men and women in equally worthwhile albeit different roles in an African cosmology and worldsense (Nzegwu, 2006; Oyewumi, 1997; Richards, 1980). In other words, African ascendant people must take control of our struggles for the sake of collective justice for African people (Hudson-Weems, 1998a). While Hudson-Weems suggests there are strong and fundamental differences between her notion of African womanism and womanism as defined by Walker, one can also argue that her version of naming does at least partly align with Walker's original definition of womanism, in that it includes a commitment "to survival and wholeness of entire people, male and female. Not a separatist [movement]" (Walker, 1983, pp. xi–xii). Hudson-Weems' (1998a) main concern is with the issue of self-naming or what she calls "a reclamation of Africana women through properly identifying our own collective struggle and acting on it" (p. 160). She further believes that the agenda of the Africana woman must be "shaped by the dictates of their past and present cultural reality. No one can be accurately defined outside of one's historical and cultural context" (Hudson-Weems, 1998b, p. 450). She goes on to claim that Africana scholars are sometimes forced to identify as feminists, to either gain legitimacy in the academy or because of a lack of a more appropriate framework that is suitable for their particular experiences. However, Busia (1993), in speaking of the need to negotiate multiple and transnational identities, calls for a more fluid, layered, and particular naming that more aptly describes the crossing of national and international boundaries in the act of naming self and other. Busia typifies the sort of complexity and dynamism within which Black women in Africa and in the diaspora wrestle, in her self-identification as

> a Ghanaian-born poet, educated in the United Kingdom, teaching in the universities of the United States of America (p. 204)...[or] as scholar, as poet, as Black, as female, as African, as an exile, as an Afro-Saxon living in Afro-America. (p. 209)

These arguments over naming Black feminism are not simply about the act of naming: They are also about defining and constructing the boundaries and possibilities for relationships *across* Black feminisms, across racial, tribal, ethnic, and national differences, as well as advocating for fundamental *human* rights. In her well-known text, *The Black Woman Cross-culturally*, Filomina Steady (1981) called for a redefinition of concepts, perspectives, and methodologies that position the transnational Black feminist researcher as an advocate for basic *human* rights throughout the world and not solely an advocate for women's rights or the rights of those in her local community. We hear echoes of that same call throughout this chapter, of African ascendant feminist acknowledgment of the oneness of male and female energy in the struggle against oppression (Wekker, 1997). These arguments are also spiritual in nature, seeing African feminism as a standpoint on human life from "a total, rather than a dichotomous and exclusive perspective" (Steady, 1981, p. 7). Steady goes on to echo a common cosmological concept in African thought that "for African women, the male is not 'the other' but part of the human same. Each gender constitutes the critical half that makes the human whole. Neither sex is totally complete in itself to constitute a unit by itself" (p. 7).

hooks (1994) welcomed these contestations in naming, perspectives, positions, and language, seeing these confrontations as less about naming and more about how these "differences [mean] that we must change ideas about how we learn" (p. 113). She continues, suggesting that "rather than fearing conflict [in naming], we have to find ways to use it as a catalyst for new thinking, for growth" (p. 113). Walker (2006) also cautions against arguments that suggest a lack of unity of purpose and proffers an alternative "combined energy" through which we can "scrutinize an oncoming foe" (p.

4). According to Walker (2006), this coming together has the potential to "rebalance the world" (p. 4) and, in the case of these contestations, help us refocus on the task before us. This task—whether historical or contemporary—requires us to (re)member that the struggle for injustice, regardless of geographical location, must include an awareness of the specific historical and cultural contexts within which oppressions are taking place, in order to identify effective frameworks with which to do the necessary work to dismantle them.

The rumblings of dissatisfaction with naming and the desire to create an organized and collective transnational Black feminist response to oppression continue today. Led by activist scholars and writers such as Steady, Collins, and Beverly Guy Sheftall, Black feminists across the globe are troubling the boundaries of the definition of feminism to describe differences in African ascendant women's experiences with racial, sexual, class, and cultural oppression. This stands to produce what Steady (1996) has called

> a more inclusive brand of feminism through which women are viewed primarily as human beings and not simply women…[that] emphasizes the totality of human experience and [is] optimistic for the total liberation of humanity….African feminism is humanistic feminism. (p. 4)

This holistic view of the African woman, in relation to her community, echoes pre-colonial African practices and values regarding the physical as well as the spiritual well-being of the community. Therefore, in contrast to the Western tendency to dichotomize the material and the spiritual, male and female, the emotional and logical, a transnational African feminism merely reflects an age-old concept of a human oneness or human wholeness, where the male is not the enemy but a co-participator in the struggle for human survival. It is important to note that this concept of oneness existed prior to the European invasion of the continent of Africa and defines the nature of African relationships and life both historically and contemporarily. Consequently, the African spiritual concept of communal well-being is more highly valued than the individualism that marks Western feminist thought. This was at least part of the tension that existed between African American feminist scholars and European American feminist scholars. We argue here that, whether conscious of this African moral value as a carryover from cultural ways of being and ways of thinking prior to the transatlantic slave trade, the pursuit of the well-being of the whole on both the continent and in the African diaspora as a means of meeting the needs of the individual and the community is a spiritual concept. Although the spiritual concept of communal wholeness and wellness prevalent in African feminism sharply contradicts the historical split between the spiritual and material so pervasive in the academy, it has been a critical part of Africana and Black feminist thought historically and continues to be pushed to the fore by scholars like Alexander (2005), Dillard (2006b), Guy-Sheftall, (1995), hooks, (2000), Hull, (2001), and Oyewumi, (1997), to name a few.

Thus, like sisters in the diaspora, continental African women scholars have not escaped the tensions present within and among African feminist scholars in defining the connections, however contentious, between versions and visions of Black feminism on the continent and in the diaspora. The well-known Ghanaian feminist writer and activist Aidoo (1998) has been criticized primarily by continental African women scholars for identifying as a feminist. Like the struggles of Black women in the United States, the accusations have to do both with the issue of naming and the critique at the epistemological level that the term feminism is a Western construct and that African women should seek empowerment through our own self-naming. The premise of the argument is that the historical realities of Western feminism do not mirror the reality of the continental African woman's historical struggles, particularly as they relate to the sufferings and current realities during and after colonialization. This argument mirrors the one made by Hudson-Weems (1995) about the need to marshal more appropriate terminology to capture Black women's experiences in the diaspora. Aidoo's defense, similar to that of her Sierra Leonean counterpart Steady, is that all men and women are feminists if they believe that the struggle for liberation for all Africans cannot be isolated from the struggle for the well-being of the African woman. Here we see again echoes of the communal versus the individual or the collective versus the self, fundamental to an African-centered cosmology.

While this discussion is by no means complete, the ethos and spirit of transnational Black feminist thought are clear: Black feminist scholars have always talked back to the exclusion of Black women's experiences in feminist research, paving the way for more global and diasporic conversations about Black women and the specialized angle of visions that we bring to the question of knowledges, cultural production, and the practices of research. The call for a naming and marshalling of Black feminism arises from a place—epistemologically, spiritually, paradigmatically—that both acknowledges and addresses the complex intersections of culture, race, class, sexualities, nation, and gender in Black women's experiences and in a way that is historically and sufficiently grounded in African ascendant ways of knowing and being. This call is reminiscent of one made over a century ago by Anna Julia Cooper, one of only two Black women to address the first Pan African Congress organized by W. E. B. Du Bois in 1900 in Paris, France. An acclaimed forerunner of Black feminism in the United States and abroad, Cooper (1892) cautioned against the expectation within Black communities generally and White feminist communities as well that the Black woman be required to fracture her identity by uplifting her gender identity over race or class. Instead, the work was and is about establishing linkages with African ascendant women globally in the struggle for elimination of all oppressions, wherever Black women are. It is about finding the sacred ground between us.

III.
Nkyimkyim (Devotion to service and willingness to withstand hardship): The spirit of an endarkened transnational feminism

> (Re)member what is dark and ancient and divine within yourself that aids your speaking. As outsiders, we need each other for support and connection and all the other necessities of living on the borders.... The oppression of women knows no ethnic nor racial boundaries, true, but that does not mean it is identical within those boundaries. (Lorde, 1984, pp. 69–71)

> Our politics initially sprang from the shared belief that black women are inherently valuable, that our liberation is a necessity not as an adjunct to somebody else's but because of our need as human persons for autonomy... We realize that only people who care enough about us to work consistently for our liberation is us... We have a very definite revolutionary task to perform, and we are ready for the lifetime of work and struggle before us. (Combahee River Collective, 1982)

The quotations above speak volumes to the possibilities of both living and creating spaces for epistemologies and methodologies that arise from the Black or endarkened feminist voices gathered here, including those voices representing multiple forms of migration to the far reaches of the globe, those who have transitioned to the spirit world, and those yet to come. What we are suggesting here is that a more globally attentive Black feminism is an endarkened feminism where its methodologies would be less about traditional academic notions of research practices and more about a sort of radical spiritual activism that encompasses the collective diversity of Black women's knowings and doings, that defines and describes our collective *ethos*, particularly given that previous definitions of Black feminism, womanism, Africana womanism, or Third World feminism may no longer hold as bridges (if they ever did) across our differences in paradigms, practices, and purposes. We have also come to know that whatever descriptions and definitions of transnational or global Black feminisms *are,* they must necessarily be "simultaneously historically specific and dynamic, not frozen in time in the form of a spectacle" (Mohanty, 1991, p. 6). What fundamentally defines and shapes an "in common" ethos and experience of Black women in the world across culture, ethnicity, national affiliation, sexual affinity, economic class and condition, and other forms of identity can be articulated by two core experiences of African ascendant women wherever you find us on the globe. These may seem both obvious and common sense, given the body of literature around Black/African/Africana feminism. However, this is our attempt to make explicit two salient knowings from which all Black women experience our lives, the spiritual consciousness from which we exist, regardless of our location on the globe. First, Black women work and live within a context of struggle against systems of oppression and exploitation, both large and small. Second, Black women work and live within a context of spirituality and the sacred, holding beliefs in something larger than ourselves. Such spiritual consciousness is what enables us as Black women to both work against that which oppresses and to find strength and even joy in the process of the work as well. And while each Black woman will experience the world in very different ways, we argue here that *this is our collective ethos or spirit as African ascendant women*. What is needed is an approach to research and inquiry that honors the wisdom, spirituality, and critical interventions of Black women's ways of knowing and being, with spirituality and sacredness being central to the work. But what is the nature or character of an endarkened feminist approach to research that can work within and against these two struggles, that can transcend our present differences, and that embraces spirituality and the sacred nature of inquiry? What might we need to consider and question as we think (and feel) our way into and toward epistemologies and methodologies that might be useful wherever we find ourselves on this globe? That is the focus of this final section.

IV.

Funtummireku-Denkyemmireku (We have a common destiny, a unity through diversity): Sacred practice, sacred dialogues and considerations for an endarkened transnational feminist methodology

> An important component of African indigenous pedagogy is the vision of the teacher [and researcher] as a selfless healer intent on inspiring, transforming, and propelling students to a higher spiritual level. (Hilliard, 1995, pp. 69–70)

Sacredness and spirituality are central to endarkened feminism. From Cooper's (1892) advocacy for the well-being of the African American community, to Steady's (1996) call for a feminism that attends to the total liberation of humanity. From Walker's (1983) definition of womanism, which includes a commitment to the survival and wholeness of entire people, male and female, to hooks's (1994) concept of the basic interdependency of life. From these voices, we can clearly see both the expectation and the relative requirement that endarkened feminist scholars bring a spiritual vision and sacred practice to bear within whatever version of Black feminism we might ascribe to, one that attends to the two common knowings for African ascendant women above. Similar to hooks (1994) and Walker (1983), Dillard (2006a) asserts that "a spiritual life is first and foremost about commitment to a way of thinking and behaving that honors principles of inter-being and interconnectedness" (p. 77). This suggests that bringing sacredness and spirituality to bear in any exploration of an endarkened transnational feminist methodology is not a frivolous exercise: It is a radical response to the need for an approach to research that honors the wisdom, spirituality, and critical interventions of transnational Black women's ways of knowing and being in research. We note again that the distinction between spirituality and the sacred is important here, particularly as it relates to research. *Spirituality* refers to having a consciousness of the realm of the spirit in one's work and its ability to transform research and teaching. When we speak of the *sacred* in endarkened feminist research, we are referring to the way the work is honored and embraced as it carried out, the reverence with which it is done, whether teaching or research.

Recently, our department offered the first doctoral seminar in education on Black feminist thought. In addition to other goals, the course was designed to be a space where an endarkened and transnational feminist epistemology and pedagogy (Dillard, 2006a) would be created, engaged, and experienced. It was about enacting a radical humanism as intervention in higher education, about a central agenda being that of becoming more fully human in all of our variations as African ascendant women (who made up the entire class). However, we were a very diverse group of Black women, representing identities, histories, and cultural affiliations that enriched our ability to engage the discussion of Black feminisms and endarkened epistemologies not simply with our minds but embodied in our methodology as well. Nationally, we had deep roots in the United States, Japan, Ghana, Nigeria, and Kenya. We had experienced the economic range from poverty to middle and upper-middle class status. We had migratory and immigration experiences that included a third of the class growing up in countries outside the United States and "becoming" citizens of the United States in adolescence, with the other two thirds having grown up in the United States (in the Pacific Northwest, the South, the North, and in both rural and urban cultural environments). We spanned the continuum of sexualities and partnering. Most important, we were deeply committed to ourselves and to doing our work as African ascendant women in the academy.

One of the first assignments in the class was a creative autobiography, where we shared stories of who we are and why we are. The course reading list represented Black and endarkened feminisms that were transnational and historical, as well as multiple in genre including films, poetry, visual art, letters, narrative, research studies, and other course syllabi. This corpus is what Bell-Scott (1994) calls *life notes*. Many of these readings are represented in the bibliography of the very book in your hands; others were suggested by the students and faculty as the course progressed. Our weekly class sessions were mostly dialogues about the readings and short presentations about content. As we were preparing this chapter (a text that we desired at the time of the class but could not find in the literature), the class became a space to engage what hooks and West (1991) call critical affirmation, the humanizing process of critique that "cuts to heal not to bleed" (Dillard, 2003). More than that, we found ourselves raising questions and critiques that explicitly showed us the difficulty of talking across our different versions of Black womanhood, even given our common "texts" and deep commitments to dialogue as sacred praxis. As the course continued, we began to see more clearly the nature and character of an endarkened transnational feminist dialogue as we engaged with each other. We also experienced the tensions and intelligibilities that still existed between us, despite our good intentions and deep commitments to dialogue. Further, we had the opportunity to engage in a cross-class dialogue with other doctoral students enrolled in a qualitative course on feminist methodologies that was being offered at the same time. These interactions further exposed the tensions and challenges of such a dialogue, particularly the racialized tensions of feminisms which often excluded feminisms of color (and certainly African ascendant feminisms) from the consciousness of White students/researchers.

What would it take to productively enter into these tensions and differences? And could explicating the character of such a dialogue help us to speak here of what an endarkened transnational feminist methodology in research might be (especially given our new understandings of the history, culture, and contestations within and among African ascendant feminisms)? A methodology that would be specific in its history and dynamic in nature? One that would be a useful way forward in the spirit of sacred praxis that Alexander (2005) called for?

The following table is our attempt to share what we learned *and* some questions we learned to raise, as authors, as members of the course, and as researchers and Sisters of the Yam. We hope it is not seen as a checklist to legitimate one's identity or research position ("I do these things and now I'm an endarkened transnational feminist researcher!"). Instead, we see it as an offering to the research community of the ways that an endarkened transnational feminist methodology may have the potential to shape a more reverent and sacred approach to inquiry that transcends our differences, our feminisms, and our lives. In this table, we put forth some considerations, categories, and questions that researchers might ask that moves towards methodology which honors an endarkened transnational feminism in research.

LEARNING TO (RE)MEMBER THE THINGS WE'VE LEARNED TO FORGET

Table 1. Considerations and Questions: Praxis in Transnational Endarkened Feminist Research

Considerations in Endarkened Transnational Feminist Research/Teaching	Some Relevant Questions for the Researcher/Teacher
On the meaning of African womanhood	
Seeks to examine the multiple intersections of oppressions of Black women relationally *and* historically	• What is or was going on here/there? • What is or was my/our relation to the lives of Black women here/there?
Sees the way that temporality shapes relative relationships between and among versions of Black womanhood, personhood	• Whose story will I tell and from what time period of "African womanhood?" • How do I struggle with the tension of the African "continent" and the "diaspora" and their relative and multiple meanings? • Have I dealt with questions of the timing (and manner) of im/migrations and the relationship to "authenticity" and naming oneself "African"?
Seeks to know Black women's experiences, contributions, cultures, and "feminisms" in all of their varieties/versions	• What do I know about African ascendant woman? • How did I gain that knowledge and what would enrich my understanding of specific versions of Black womanhood or endarkened feminisms? • How can this knowledge get in the way of my seeing and understanding the vision and version of African ascendant feminism under study?
Embodies responsibility and respect, different than the cult of womanhood	• How have I prepared to study the lives of Black women differently than I would for other women? • What would show that I respect the particularities of her understandings and embodiment of cultural norms, geographies, and traditions?
On the sacred nature of experience	
Seeks to recognize multiple experiences outside of one's own	• In what ways does the story I'm hearing (or the text I'm reading) map on to my experience and knowings? • In what ways is it different? • How do I hold those differences as sacred (with reverence), without judgment or denial in their difference?
Recognizes that you can never be the "expert" on another's experience and, thus, must move yourself out of the way to make room for the liberation of others	• What does their experience mean to them? • Can I hear and imagine the depth of the meaning of their experiences and empathize without trying to "save" another? • What does their story mean to me and what emotions/memories does it evoke? How do my emotions mediate (or distort) their intended meaning?

Continued on following page

THE IMPORTANCE OF NAMING

Considerations in Endarkened Transnational Feminist Research/Teaching	Some Relevant Questions for the Researcher/Teacher
On recognizing *African community and landscapes*	
Shares the need for alliance and reliance: *I am because we are*	• Where are the recognitions and engagements in this work of an endarkened womanhood that moves between and even beyond nation, culture, sexualities, economic class, language, and so on?
Recognizes the dynamic and shifting landscapes and configurations of identity and social location of groups	• How does what I thought I knew about this individual/group match what I am hearing from engagements with him/her/them? • Where are the places and people who could provide disconfirming data? Have I sought this out?
Is committed to knowing one another's stories through sustained relationship for the purposes of bettering conditions that may not mirror our own	• Can I rest in that place where it is not all/always about me? • Are humility, sacrifice, and selflessness at the center of my desire to "know"?
On engaging *body, mind, and spirit*	
Makes *space* for mind, body, and spirit to be a part of the work	• How have I sought knowledge at a level of intimacy and wholeness (beyond the mind), at the level of the senses, the sensual, and the spiritual? • What questions have I asked of myself and another that move toward connections of our spirit? • What would happen if I "went there"?
Is reciprocal, as every person is both teacher and taught, changing as we know the other and the other knows us	• In what ways are my views of research shifting as a result of my research? • What "lessons" have I learned from others in this inquiry? What are the lessons they've learned from me? • When someone reads this work, how will they know that I approached this project with reverence?
Requires radical openness and vulnerability	• In what ways have I "shown up" for this inquiry? • How am I hiding in fear of what I am, what I don't know or misunderstand, or who the other is or what they know?

These considerations and questions suggest that, as we work to live and theorize from and through endarkened transnational epistemologies and methodologies, we must also shift our attention and engagement to embrace a more sacred (reverent) understanding of our relationships with and in endarkened spaces of womanhood and feminisms. We must go beyond employing or engaging our methodologies: We must *be* differently, asking relevant (and reverent) questions of our practice and of ourselves. The categories and considerations are discussed in brief here.

On the meaning of African womanhood. Endarkened transnational research acknowledges that the lives of African ascendant women are intertwined and interconnected, given our shared legacy of oppressions on the African continent and in the African diaspora. This awareness does not discount the ways that temporality shapes Black women's experiences (Okpalaoka, 2009). Neither does this awareness discount the notion that there are variations of feminisms that reflect the varied nuances of oppression manifested in women's specific historical, cultural, and geographical locations. The disruption of African ascendant peoples' lives through enslavement, colonization, and apartheid across temporal and geographical boundaries only serves to connect us across these boundaries. A respect for the particularities of Black women's understandings and embodiment of cultural norms, geographies, and traditions must be reflected in the research and work of inquiry.

On the sacred nature of experience. At the core of Black feminism (Collins, 2000; Steady, 1996) and endarkened feminism (Dillard, 2006a) is the recognition of the expertise that Black women acquire through our lived experiences and specific to our lived conditions. An approach to endarkened transnational feminist research is one in which the researcher and the researched are engaged in a mutually humbling experience, where each understands our limitations in speaking for the other. An endarkened transnational feminist epistemology and methodology recognize that there are multiple experiences outside of one's own. Therefore, the role of researcher as expert will serve only to hinder the liberation of those with whom we engage in research and the cultural and spiritual knowledge that is inherently valuable to both of us as human and spiritual beings.

On recognizing African community and landscapes. The South African concept of Ubuntu ("I am because we are") and the Ghanaian (Akan) concept of Funtummireku-denkyemmireku ("We have a common destiny") embody the need to recognize the powerful and omnipresent role of community from an endarkened transnational perspective. We are arguing here that while Western thought seeks to elevate the individual above the community, researchers committed to an endarkened transnational feminist praxis are also committed to knowing another's stories through both telling one's own and through the sustained relationship in community that such dialogue requires. While the notion of Ubuntu is taken up in more detail in the next chapter, from such a standpoint, part of our work as researchers is to improve life conditions that may not mirror our own. In other words, while we recognize the specifics of the oppressions within and amongst African ascendant women, as long as some form of oppression is present within our collective reality, we all must engage in the struggle for freedom from oppression and to achieve full humanhood. We are in a collective struggle for liberation regardless of the specifics of our conditions. An endarkened transnational feminist praxis works beyond self to recognize the dynamic and shifting landscapes and configurations of identity and social location of groups.

On engaging body, mind, and spirit. Endarkened transnational feminist research is research that makes space for mind, body, and spirit to be a part of the work. It invites the whole person of the researcher and the whole person of the researched into the work, knowing that the mind, body, and spirit are intertwined in their functions of maintaining the well-being of the individual and community. The place of the sacred in endarkened and transnational feminisms requires radical openness, especially on the part of the researcher, who understands deeply that her or his humanity is linked with that of the people with whom he or she studies. The act of sharing with those who have been silenced and marginalized is a spiritual task that embodies a sense of humility and intimacy. Furthermore, a sense of reciprocity is fundamental from this epistemological space, a sense that the researcher and the researched are changed in the process of mutual teaching and learning the world together.

As we end this chapter, two things are clear. First, this exploration of endarkened transnational feminisms affirms the sacred praxis of Black women on the continent and throughout the diaspora. This chapter is our contribution to the collective legacy of struggle and spirit, to "write all the things I should have been able to read" (Walker, 1983, p. 13). However, this exploration of endarkened transnational feminisms also points to the ways that the paradigms and epistemologies that have been marshaled in qualitative research have still not answered the deeper spiritual questions that undergird many cultural phenomena, the persistent social problems of equity and justice, the difficulties of community and solidarity, and the complex nature of identity and personhood.

Given an African cosmology and epistemology, the authors strongly resist attempts to predict the future of the field of Black/endarkened feminist thought, as past, present, and future are implicated and embraced in our current existence, not as separate but as part of the same circle of time. As we have examined the history of Black feminisms on both sides of the water to arrive at a place where we believe a more transnational endarkened feminism is necessity and offers the research community possibility, one thing is clear: That attention to paradigms, epistemologies, and praxis that also center the spiritual and sacred nature of qualitative research is the necessary way forward.

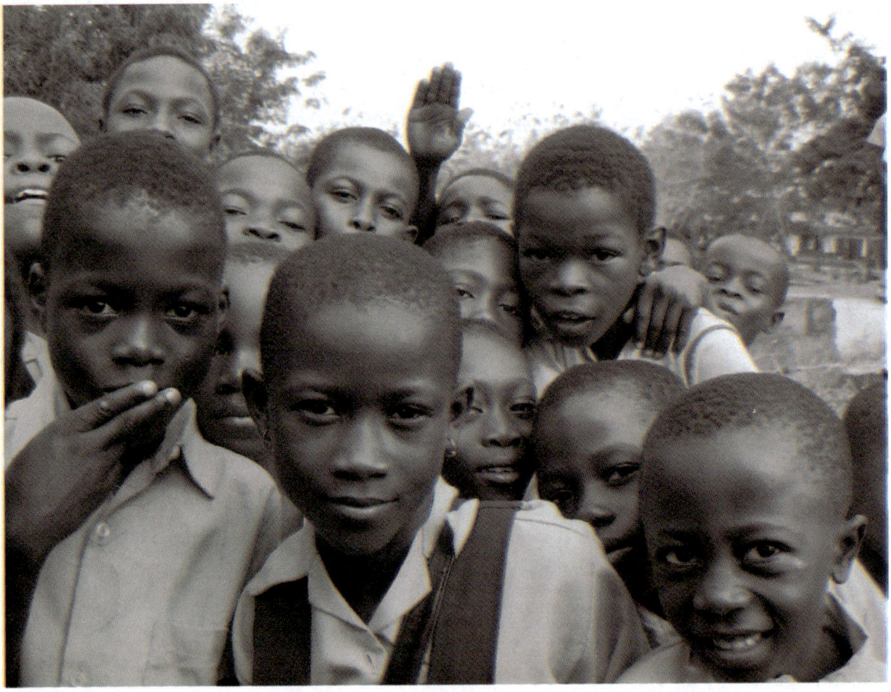

CHAPTER SIX

Pedagogies of Community Are Pedagogies of the Spirit

Living Ubuntu

Introduction: To change the energy in the room

After a friend of mine had a serious stroke last fall, I was told of a book that might help me better understand how to support her recovery and to know what to do with the overwhelming cacophony of concern and care coming to me from hundreds in her national and international community. Trying to stay hopeful during the weeks she was in the intensive care unit, I quickly ordered this book and was thrilled when it came in its promised three days. The book was entitled *My Stroke of Insight* by Jill Bolte Taylor, a former brain scientist who'd also suffered a stroke. During Taylor's recovery time in the hospital when she was unable to use her voice to speak, she found herself being much more attuned to energy, "sensing" rather than always speaking when a person entered the room, particularly the nurses. She could sense whether the nurse was present to her as a patient or was thinking about getting off early from work or some other problem of the day. She could sense the nurse's disposition in the way her food was mindlessly placed on the tray, in the way the nurse pulled open the blinds or in how the nurse listened (or not) to what she was communicating with her body, mind, and spirit. She could simply *feel* the energy of the nurse. Mostly, she could feel whether the energy of those around her assisted in her healing or literally made her sicker, whether it served the good or served to bring negativity or grief to her. So she asked someone to make her a sign which they posted above the door to her room. It simply said the following: "Please be responsible for the energy that you bring into this room." And that is how we might look at the profound work of being teachers and researchers: As being responsible for the energy we bring to the space and practice, to what we bring as teachers and researchers to our work and our community of students and partners in research. Teaching asks us to be present, to care, and to be able to respond to the students and others within our purview: Being able to do so with all who gather, with care and love for the energy we bring to the endeavor, characterizes our response-ability.

In many African ascendant people (particularly those of us living in diaspora), I have sensed a deep desire to be responsible for the energy we bring into the various rooms we occupy. But given a history fraught with exclusions, we also feel a sense of responsibility to literally shift and transform the energy in those rooms by our very presence. In the classrooms where we teach. In the scores of meetings that we attend. On the committees which we serve. In the spaces and relationships we have with family, friends, and colleagues. In the memories we implicitly and explicitly share in our daily interactions, that also tell volumes about the meanings we attach to identity, culture, tradition, and life. These are memories of becoming, memories always in formation (Alexander, 2005; Appiah, 2006; Strong-Wilson, 2008; Trinh, 1989), in consistent and constant renegotiation of what we've been, are, and might be. And, for African people, they are memories deeply rooted in and committed to the spirit of community. This chapter focuses on the deep meanings of our commitments to a spirit of community from an African feminist spiritual perspective. Here, I want to put spirituality to work, theorizing teaching and research as commitments to a spirit of community at the level of endarkened feminist epistemology and culture, in other words, at the level of who we are, why we are, and what we can be as African ascendant women particularly and people more generally. This is the very level of energy that Jill Bolte Taylor suggests that we are responsible for, with the ultimate goal being that of becoming more fully human (Freire, 1970). However, there is also a profound assumption within that goal that may unfortunately itself be revelatory and revolutionary to some, even in this twenty-first century: That is, that African ascendant people are human, not accidentally but on purpose and for a purpose (Moyers & Pellett, 1988; Fanon, 1967; Vanzant, 1993). So it stands to reason that (re)membering African personhood is part of the existential work that must be undertaken in teaching, not just by African ascendants but by everyone.

I also place the commitment to a spirit of community at the center of this discussion of teaching and research as a counter-commitment to the current use of community as mostly rhetorical, a virtual commitment, a lion with no teeth. Instead, I want to engage a commitment to the spirit of community as the African spiritual mandate that it is, raising possibilities for rethinking teaching and research as spaces that are— or can become—deeply embedded in cultural memory and imbued with the intention of being responsible for the energy that we bring to the room as teachers and researchers.

The spirit of *Ubuntu*: A commitment to community

For this discussion of the central place of community in African spiritual frameworks, I draw on the African concept of *Ubuntu*. *Ubuntu* can be understood as a symbiotic and cooperative relationship between people that provides the basis for a spiritual reading of community and the acts of community-making from an African standpoint. According to Battle (2009),

> [Ubuntu] comes from a linguistic group of sub-Saharan languages known as Bantu. Both words Ubuntu and Bantu can be recognized by the common root of –*ntu* (human). The prefix *ba*- denotes the plural form for humanity. In short Ubuntu means personhood. A further etymological foundation for –*ntu* can be translated as *being*, that is human being. In the spirituality common to sub-Saharan Africa, there is a direct relationship between human being and God's being. Ubuntu, therefore, also includes a theological understanding in which all beings are known through the category of personhood. (p. 3, emphasis his)

Said operationally, *Ubuntu* suggests that each individual's full personhood is ideally expressed in relationship with others. It is only through such expression within and in relation to the collective that individuality itself is expressed. One can immediately see the serious contradiction with Western assumptions of personhood that focus primarily on the individual, assumptions that also tend to place at their core Whiteness, patriarchy, and heterosexuality as the norm against which all non-Western assumptions of what it means to be human are measured (Battle, 2009; Krog, 2010; Wynter, 1990). But from the perspective of *Ubuntu*, a person depends on others to *be* a person, to be human, belonging to a wholeness greater than he/she can ever achieve alone. *Ubuntu* then is the "*interdependence* of persons for the exercise, development, and fulfillment of their potential to be both individuals and community (Battle, 2009, p. 3, emphasis mine). Battle goes on to say that extended family, an important pillar in African communities and societies, provides one's first site of living *Ubuntu*. Through extended families, a person becomes able to live an extended and expanded existence, "not only through those related by blood, kinship, or marriage, but through humanity itself, conceived as a family one joins at birth and in which no one is a stranger" (pp. 3–4). Desmond Tutu, the reknowned archbishop from South Africa, describes the countenance of a person who embraces or embodies a commitment to *Ubuntu*, a description that serves as a helpful example in imagining the spirit of this commitment in teaching and research:

> A person with Ubuntu is open and available to others, affirming of others, does not feel threatened that others are able and good, for he or she has a proper self-assurance that comes

from knowing that he or she belongs in a greater whole and is diminished when others are humiliated or diminished, when others are tortured or oppressed. (Tutu, 1999, p. 31)

While we see can see these commitments to *Ubuntu* within the work of some African diasporic scholars (and others who marshal spiritually centered philosophies of teaching and learning), I will point to several as exemplars. Asa Hilliard (1995) focuses on the centrality of community and spirituality in African worldsense and provides extant models for African-centered pedagogies, curriculum development, and frameworks based in community. Joy James (1993) argues for the theoretical and the pragmatic usefulness of Pan-African community, highlighting the ways that community is unbounded by temporal or physical limits. She argues that Africans belong to the African community, even when not residing in a predominately African community. In this way, the notion of community continues to be more expansive and generative given research connections made within the African world and beyond. Joyce King (2005) situates teaching and research practice not as the luxury of academics or as alienated activity but as *central* to the African community. In her ground-breaking edited volume *Black Education: A Transformative Research and Action Agenda for the New Century* (commissioned by the American Educational Research Association), she poignantly illustrates the functions and challenges of creating and nurturing community for Black people, particularly in education. Valerie Kinloch's work on community, represented in her award-winning book *Harlem on Our Minds: Place, Race, and the Literacies of Urban Youth* (2010) focuses attention on contemporary issues of Black community, literacies, and the outcomes and influences of place on creating and sustaining Black community in these multicultural times. Parker Palmer (1998) suggests that the fundamental goal of teaching and learning is the creation of community, both in one's inner life and with others. He also has spoken to the central role of spirituality in educational practice (1993). Ladson-Billings (2000) specifically contrasts the concept of individualism and the elevation of the individual mind prevalent in Western thought with the African notion of *Ubuntu* in relation to inquiry and qualitative research. With the exception of Ladson-Billings, most of these scholars do not explicitly or specifically name *Ubuntu* as the theoretical framework marshaled to do their work. However, embedded within each piece is the commitment to *Ubuntu,* to community as a way of life, a way to imbue and enliven our dialogues and relationships with meaning centered in African ways of knowing and being. Battle (2009) puts forth five points that undergird the deeper meanings of *Ubuntu* and that are helpful to the discussion here, as they provide a possible framework for thinking about and committing to deeper engagements of community in our teaching and learning and to ways that resonate with and provide space for African cultural memories and spirituality to be invited into our endeavors. Further, such a framework would open a space of reconciliation and (re)membering what we've learned to forget about African personhood as well. As a way of being human, a commitment to *Ubuntu* also provides an alternative framework through which we might interrogate and examine our teaching practices in substantive ways, in ways that move through and beyond the limitations of race and identity to more spiritual notions of identity, those that typify identity as a space to live spirituality. According to Battle (2009), these five points of *Ubuntu* are as follows:

1. Self-identity is not optimally formed through competition but rather through cooperation.
2. Being in community requires skill to see it and to create it.
3. The notion of *Ubuntu* expands Western horizons, providing a counter-practice of community, rooted deeply in African cultural productions.
4. *Ubuntu* deepens our spirituality.
5. The development of *Ubuntu* also requires the development of a communal self, both of which require practice. (p. 6)

Through cultural memories of teaching and research, the following sections seek to make more explicit what a commitment to *Ubuntu* both within and outside of formal classroom settings might look like. The first memory is illustrative of Battle's points 1 and 2 above, that is that self-identity is best formed in cooperation vs. competition and that community requires skill for us to see it and create it. The second memory highlights Battle's points 3 and 4, that *Ubuntu* expands Western notions of community which in turn, deepens our spirituality. The final memory serves to embrace Battle's point that a communal self is fundamental to *Ubuntu* and requires practice to develop.

I have several hopes in sharing these cultural memories. The first is that they might be illustrative of the possibilities of pedagogies of *Ubuntu*, serving as examples of the intentional practices of/in community with myself and others that help us to see how our self-identities are also deeply informed by one another (and too often deformed and misinformed by one another as well). A second hope is that the reader might understand *Ubuntu* beyond its rhetorical goodness to the deeper, messier, often fearful places that a commitment to *Ubuntu* in teaching and research might actually take us and to the real possibilities on the other side of those experiences. Finally, my hope is that the reader might also (re)member and recognize his/her own practices of *Ubuntu* (or question the lack thereof), opening a space for educational practices to be informed and possibly transformed through this discussion. Thus, this examination is about asking new questions of our tried-and-true methods, fundamental questions that might help us not only shift the energy in our classrooms but be responsible for it as well. The questions to ask ourselves as teachers and scholars? *In what ways do my teaching and research practices embody a commitment (named or unnamed) to creating a spirit of community, of* Ubuntu? Maybe more importantly, *How would the African ascendant people gathered together in classroom or project see and feel my commitment to* Ubuntu?

The elusiveness of community: The case of spirit, race, and dialogue

Too seldom do opportunities arise for graduate women scholars to engage in conversations and explorations (within the context of graduate school) about the meaning and wisdom of women's ways of knowing and being. But creating community for women generally and women of color particularly cannot happen without such engagements if one of the end goals is the ability to live and work cooperatively across our differences. I focus here on the wisdom and development of a group of multi-racial/ethnic women's voices that arose from a year-long doctoral seminar entitled *Spirit, Race, and Dialogue* (SRD). This course was conceived and co-taught by myself, an African American faculty member, and another colleague and dear friend who is European American faculty member. It was also guided by our deep and very different theoretical approaches and cultural commitments to spirituality, to endarkened/Black feminisms, anti-racism, narrative and qualitative research, and to transformative critical pedagogies in teacher education collectively. Together, my colleague and I developed four core questions that we explored with our students in various ways throughout our year together:

- Why are we here?
- Why do so many of us feel a sense of angst and limitation, especially as teachers and researchers who care deeply about social justice and multiculturalism?
- Is it possible to heal ourselves, our work, our understandings of each other, and our research, particularly around race?
- Is there something more to living as academics than "jumping through hoops" and how do we make a space in our academic lives to do *that* work?

Further the seminar was designed to be both progressive and cumulative. During fall quarter, we began with "The Conversation," where we read, studied, and engaged considerable time and energy developing theoretical and conceptual understandings of race, spirituality, and dialogue. This was collective time, spent mostly as a large group. Winter quarter we titled "Living Ground." This was a time for living and experiencing one another through a series of spiritual, cultural, and explicitly racially based experiences. We continued to study, write, reflect and engage, this time in small, cross-racial groups. Spring quarter focused on "Witnessing Experience." It was designated as our writing quarter and used as research space to analyze our experiences of fall and winter quarters, and their connections to our teaching and research lives.

A central commitment of the SRD seminar was to explicitly engage theories and texts centered on spirituality and feminisms that might help us unpack our uncomfortabilities with race and identity *across* our racial/ethnic differences. However, during spring quarter, we also engaged in necessary conversations and dialogues that were conducted *within* our racial/ethnic heritage groups. In other words, through our actions and pedagogies as instructors, we made explicit the importance of separate identity work particularly within European and African ascendant groups. These conversations and engagements were led by the faculty member of the same racial identity group. We held three of these intra-group conversations, most followed by a regathering of the entire seminar group for discussions afterward. However, these intra-group dialogues (especially as they related to the concepts of race and to healing the lived experience of racism) were difficult in different ways across racial and ethnic groups. They were also critically affirming within each group and a space of reconciliation and (re)membering. For the African ascendant women, these conversations of "sisters of the yam" (hooks, 1993) opened a way for new Black women's wisdom to arise that created spaces where we could clearly see the importance of Black identity, knowledge, cultural productions, and spirituality in informing both the difficult conversations around racism and sexism and the influence on/in our academic lives (Okpalaoka & Dillard, 2011).

However, key to the "success" of this course was its ability to center and encourage cooperation and dialogue across racial/ethnic heritage groups, even in its difficulty. I want to share here some of the common threads of identity and the difficulties inherent in fostering cooperation in dialogue versus engaging competition and fear. These are the cornerstones of the spirit of an *Ubuntu* call for self-identity as a spiritual and cultural way of being: They were also cornerstones of the SRD course. And this course brought up the rather elusive nature of community, the need to develop skills to witness community, and the work needed to also create it.

The readings in SRD focused on exploring the landscapes of our inner lives in all of their diversity. From bell hooks's call to be "all about love" (2000) to Alice Walker's call that "we are the ones we've been waiting for" (2006), the dialogue was personal and very intimate, raising often first-time questions about race and self-identity not just to/of the other but maybe more importantly to/of the self. Exploring these inner spaces was sometimes painful and often difficult to traverse, requiring us to uncover memories that implicated beloved families and histories, our cultural understandings, our racialized experiences, and unexamined notions of class and gender. Many in the class (from both Black and White racial and cultural groups) described what were referred to as psychic assaults, those places where as individuals and members of groups, we have been disconnected from or distorted through our "race," cultures, and heritages. But some of the consequences of disconnection were also personal and individual: They were places where we ourselves had intentionally disconnected or distorted ourselves to survive these assaults. The rather intimate in-class dialogues helped us to see these distortions, allowing us to deepen our understanding of what one student referred to as our "stuck places": Our hurts, our desires for validation and love, our too-quick and often ugly judgments when what we were expecting (from family, friends, and each other) did not come. In turn, this honest examination deepened our understanding and helped us to develop a certain empathy with our families, friends, those within our racial groups and outside of them. But it also led us to more "stuck places."

Some of the new stuck places were located in our lack of skills to productively read and understand the deeper concepts of race and culture (our own and others) and our inability and lack of knowledge oftentimes to do so. In our reading of Kwame Appiah's (1992) book, *In My Father's House: Africa in the Philosophy of Culture,* we discussed the importance of knowing another through individual and collective cultural memory as a prerequisite to reading culture productively and thus being able to be truly present with one another. But even by the end of the year-long course, there was still difficulty in this reading as a community. Part of this difficulty was like a deep chasm, a lack of understanding between the racial groups. The European ascendants had little experience with being or feeling "raced," and the African ascendant group had lifetimes of experiences with the deleterious effects of race and extensive racism historically, structurally, and spiritually. Although this lack of understanding was a common, even everyday, experience for the African ascendant women, it was a space of ignorance, denial, and even anger for most of the European ascendant women. What seemed most difficult for the White women was to recognize their own ignorance about race and racism, to not speak with "expertise" about racism that they had not lived, and to learn to listen and be comfortable with Black women as experts on their own experience without the need for their interpretation of that experience. Engaging in this way (what one of the White students called "heart open listening") was difficult to balance fundamentally with talking about/through the concept of race. We turned to Thich Nhat Hanh's ideas about listening deeply, in *Teachings on Love* (1998). The reason? Explicit talk about race was highlighting the imbalance in positioning as we'd known it, particularly for Black and White people in the U.S. Those who had traditionally held privileged knowledge and expertise saw that advantage turned on its ear, and the weight of experience with race and racism became the 500-lb. elephant in the room. Frustration increased over time between both groups, with the African ascendant women suffering not only through our identities and cultural memories but through the very weight of racism. And the inability to resolve this situation raised serious questions in our minds and hearts of the possible limits of cross-cultural talk of race. In "public" talk of race, who is at the center? Who is marginalized? Who gets to speak? Who remains silenced? The talk and listening we needed was something much more reciprocal and relational than we seemed able to do as Black and White women together. It was a type of talk and listening that we tried desperately to develop in our large group but that was fundamentally incompatible with the concept of race from the spiritual commitment to community that we were trying to develop and build. In other words, to practice *Ubuntu*, we had to be able to differentiate ourselves and maintain a distinct identity but also be in community with all gathered. That was essential to being response-able. And as Battle (2009) suggests "the very act of self-differentiation is itself the beauty of Ubuntu. You cannot know you are unique or beautiful or intelligent without the reference points of a community in which such attributes become intelligible" (p. 8). But still, by the end of the course, we hadn't found our way back to one another in a way that moved us beyond feeling ethnicity and race as the essence of our being human.

In the end, the African ascendant students with whom I worked came to understand a lesson that helped to serve our liberation, that moved the class towards a deeper embrace of *Ubuntu*. Part of what was learned from the tensions that existed across ethnicity and race for these women was the deeper realization that we were African ascendant women. *Black women*. No matter how hard we tried, how many experiences we shared of the ways that race and racism served as oppressive forces within Black life and in all of our lives, the call to community was one that required, as the traditional Negro spiritual tells us, to "study war no more." Instead, the affirmation of Blackness, of womanness, of spirit as the common ground led us to realize our larger purpose: *"I heal myself so that others can heal."* The work became not trying to convince or push our European sisters to believe that our experiences were "real" or truthful or needed to be presented solely to please them. Instead, there developed a deepened desire to be whole and recognize our being (in the past, present, and future) as a transcendent identity, one that moves through and beyond the limits of racial identity to that which is spiritual and common in all human beings. We read and studied bell hooks's (1993) *Sisters of the Yam* and *All about Love: New Visions* (2000). We even named our group Sisters of the Yam (or SOTY, as we are now (re)membered), as our unabashed commitment to an African heritage. Beyond class time and assignments, we met regularly to affirm our spirituality as African ascendant scholars and to critique the stuck places within *ourselves*. Then we brought those selves back to the table in dialogue with our European sisters, moving through our anger and frustrations in what continued to seem like a never-ending dance on the surface of their lives when talking about race. But our collective perspective as Black women had shifted to the place where we could see that dance without judgment but with love. What we as Black women realized was that through affirming ourselves as *individuals* in the context of that larger group, we came to create what Palmer (1998) and Battle (2009) describe as the community itself, both within our selves and beyond ourselves:

> Ubuntu …shapes the vision for how the relationship between persons creates a third entity. In other words, Ubuntu helps us see the complementarity between the individual and the community…[it] helps us guard against the unfortunate tendency of approaching relationships as what one person can get out of the others, thereby killing the opportunity for the third life to be born, the life of the community. (Battle, 2009, p. 8)

In other words, the African ascendant women realized that our identities—as Black/female/teachers/scholars/etc.—were too often based in fear, especially in the academic context. That fear is characterized by what comedian Wanda Sykes comically but poignantly refers to as an oft-heard admonishment by her mother that she behave in a particular way around White people. This is an admonishment echoed by scores of Black mothers, albeit in varying words and ways: *"White people are looking at you."* As we explored cultural memories, unpacked them, and examined them, we realized that attempting to please White people, to not have them see us as different than they are, to rein ourselves in was the operating principle we had worked within, as academic women. But we also realized that seeing ourselves as the spirits that we are allowed us to see ourselves more clearly and our European colleagues more clearly as well. That is what embracing an *Ubuntu* commitment to community does: It helps us to see ourselves bigger than our identities based on race, culture, and gender and then literally *reorients* our visions of ourselves and of others. And as one of the African ascendant sisters shared, if building and creating community is really centered unconditionally in love, "it will carry us through." Yes, we may have to help each other through the process. Yes, there will be stuck places. Yes, it will be emotional. "But if done in love and with commitment," she smiled, "we'll all be okay on the other side."

Wherever I am, that's where God is: Explorations of community beyond the West

A conscious commitment to *Ubuntu* is also a commitment to becoming. Teaching and research are not simply in the acts of preparing lectures, constructing what we see as an exciting curriculum or walking into the university or the school: They are about *becoming the school*. The former actions assume or suggest that at some point, we have actually left the school: Becoming the school suggests that schooling and teaching are always already within us: We *are* the school. And as Palmer (1998) further suggests, "Good teaching cannot be reduced to technique; good teaching comes from the identity and integrity of the teacher" (p. 10). If we adhere to this statement, then our work as professors and teachers is about becoming the school, enlarging and enlivening our bodies, minds, and spirits such that we become an offering to our students that enriches the very space of community with and within them, that changes the energy in the room (Taylor, 2009). This is what Fernandes (2003) describes as a living divinity, "a radical form of liberation of the divine—within ourselves, our communities, our world" (p. 116). This is especially true of our ethnic and cultural distinctions, which, contrary to many discourses, are valuable and central to a commitment to *Ubuntu*: We *need* the distinctions of another to make the whole community. As Battle (2009) states: "In our God given differences we are called to realize our need of one another....Persons and governments cannot stipulate God's preference of persons on the basis of race" (p. 66). Thus, a commitment to *Ubuntu* sees diversity as an asset and not a deficit.

However, embracing *Ubuntu* is also a commitment to alleviating poverty, whether intellectual, physical, spiritual, or economic (Cone, 1990; Gutierrez, 2003; Tutu, 1999; West, 1994). Although most liberation theologies are based in a practice of spirituality of the poor, Fernandes (2003) also cautions against seeing the call to community as a rescue of the poor from themselves but instead an opportunity to be in community with others and to embrace the opportunity to be the taught and not the teacher:

> The lesson was not that the poor were an idealized embodiment of virtue, but that their struggles for survival and transformation provided them with a form of spiritual wisdom which more privileged individuals needed to learn from. (Fernandes, 2003, p. 116)

Such spiritual wisdom and strength must be seen in our formation of community as arising from those who have experienced subordination and subjugation. We saw this in the story of the SRD course. Such strength and wisdom provide a vision of community and transformation garnered in the face of tremendous odds. If we return to the idea of teachers being the school from which students learn (among many "schools" in our lifetimes), we also return to the notion of a spirituality and pedagogy that are embodied, that are constructed with/in community. Not necessarily religious, this spirituality is a deep commitment to being in the world, but not of it, to being unafraid of people of different faith traditions, races, or cultures and seeing their lives as manifestations of the diversity of life that is necessary to more deeply understand and bless your own.

In the following section, I bear witness, through cultural memory, to the ways that being in community can deepen one's spirituality, can help one embrace a deeper and embodied commitment to Ubuntu. These memories arise from a life-changing trip made to El Salvador in 1987. I traveled with a small group of five persons representing various religions and faith communities from the Washington, Oregon, and Idaho tri-state region. Our activities were an organized part of a larger delegation of about 500 United States citizens who had worked extensively in our local contexts on behalf of social justice, self-determination, and more peaceful solutions to the war-torn and dismal economic situation in El Salvador at that time. Further, our goal was to push for a more just and humane response and involvement from the government and peoples of the United States of America.[1]

The reader should know that, with the exception of two well-known Catholic leaders Father Trini and Raphael, I use pseudonyms for all of the Salvadorans whom I met during my stay in El Salvador. This is done to protect them from political repercussions even today. It was also done in the event that our writings had been confiscated by the police or airport security. I tore my journal into pieces and taped it to my body before going through airport security in order to be able to bear witness to the situation in El Salvador at that time.

So these particular excerpts were selected to illustrate how the threads of spirituality, community, and activist praxis actually look in direct experiences with people whose languages, cultures, and conditions are different from one's own. But they were also selected to use these texts to "create dangerously," as Danticat (2010) so poignantly urges us to do and which I take up in the final chapter of this book. Further, like the fundamental notions of base-Christian communities outlined in Rodriguez and Fortier (2007), these experiences might help us as teachers and researchers

---

1 One of the purposes for participants on this trip was to literally put our bodies on the line as "human shields" in the middle of this Salvadoran "civil" war. Because the U.S. and Salvadoran government knew of the presence of U.S. citizens and other foreign nationals in particular communities throughout El Salvador, large-scale mortaring, bombing, and kidnappings were less likely to occur while we were present amidst the people of El Salvador. As a strategy of solidarity, the SHARE organizers were responsible for rotating thousands of citizens from all over the world on a consistent and steady basis in and out of Salvadoran communities throughout the late 1980s.

to more closely: 1) review the realities of the world; 2) reflect on them, finding meaning and explanation, and 3) proceed with some kind of action (p. 73). These ideas are embodied in Freire's (1970) very powerful notion of critical consciousness as a part of praxis and pedagogies of the oppressed as well. Most importantly, these experiences provide a context for the types of deep spiritual conversions that are available in community and that I suggest are critical for teachers and researchers who authentically and responsibly research and teach in the spirit of *Ubuntu* as a conscious and intentional process. It is the sort of conversion implied in the following description by Gutierrez (2003):

> A conversion is the starting point of every spiritual journey. It involves a break with the life lived up to that point; it is a prerequisite for entering the kingdom....It presupposes also, and above all, that one decides to set out on a new path....A conversion is not something that is done once and for all. It entails a development, even a painful one, that is not without uncertainties, doubts, and temptations to turn back on the road less traveled...[One's] faith deepens with the passage of time. To believe in God is more than simply to profess God's existence; it is to enter into communion with God and—the two being inseparable—with our fellow human beings as well. And this adds up to *a process*. (pp. 95–96, emphasis mine)

Part of the call here in bringing a more conscious spirituality to teaching and research is about attending not just to the intellectual openings in our understanding of one another and our practice but to the spiritual ones as well. It is about being willing to be transformed and "taught" by all that we encounter and recognizing these encounters as purposeful and expansive, both in the very ways that we *think* about our relationship to others in the world as well as how we *feel* about them...

San Salvador, El Salvador, 1987

March 20, 1987

We arrived in El Salvador with little drama. Had an orientation with Father Trini, a Salvadoran Catholic priest. He helped us to understand what we might see while we're here, how things will work. And several things he said really struck me. He said: "The hope of the people is great. They want peace to reconstruct their lives." The other: "We hear about people who commit suicide in the U.S. Our people don't do this. We're not thinking about dying because we're just trying to live." Wow.

Because we're a small delegation of only five, we will be going out to stay a few days in a repopulated comunidad called Tres Ceibas. The people at Tres Ceibas were originally displaced people from refugee camps and were accustomed to working the land all day. [So], they wanted deeply to continue to work the land, anywhere. They arranged with some people in a church to get permission to move to this land, Tres Ceibas. They developed economic projects like growing tomatoes and corn to sell and, mostly, to supplement their diets. They also tend beehives. But they're on the list to be dealt with by the government for trying to make a life for themselves....

When we arrived at Tres Ceibas, we found simple homes and the welcoming arms of children and mostly women. Many of the men have fled to escape death when there are raids of the camps by the police, who come dressed as civilians. And there are also informants. I must be careful with my words.

I am writing while sitting on a rock, talking to two Salvadoran women. And tears are streaming down my face. A gorgeous bass-sounding boom. And another. And another. As I sit here, in what's supposed to be a non-conflict zone, I can hear bombs dropping in the very near distance. No doubt, people are being killed and their homelands ruined. Abuela says: "Many nights there are bombs that come down like rain." And now I hear them nearly every 15 minutes. Martin says: "The democracy of Duarte is this (the sound of the bombs)." In the newspaper at home, I remember reading about who is fighting here. They're called guerillas. It's portrayed as a war of capitalists vs. communists, not unlike the rhetoric that surrounded our reasons for being in Vietnam [and now in Iraq]. But what I am learning? "Guerillas" are the name of people simply fighting for their rights to live as human beings.

March 21, 1987

Last night, we knelt at the 14 stations of the cross. The kids built gorgeous crosses out of little pieces of wood and found objects and, with us, visited all 14 stations. We knelt and prayed for a better situation, for improved lives for all of us. And whatever spirit is, it was there with us. It was beautiful and so powerful. My words don't capture it at all.

...I learned today that Blacks are not allowed to live in El Salvador.[2] I suppose it's okay for us to visit? Salvadoran people say they like having us visit. Does this raise any red flags, USA? We call this a democracy in action, one which we support? Now I understand why I am a "star attraction" amongst the group since we arrived: Black folks are absent on purpose. My pelo (hair) is a big deal.

---

[2] The racial/ethnic history of African ascendant people in El Salvador helps to explain the invisibility of Black people in El Salvador. El Salvador is the only country in Central America that has no visible presence of people of African heritage. Part of the historical explanation is because of its relative inaccessibility to the Atlantic Ocean and thus the transatlantic slave trade route. However, President Martinez (1931–1944), who seized power of El Salvador in a palace coup, was also an admirer of fascism and ordered on-going massacres of indigenous Salvadorans. At that time, he also created a racial law to keep Blacks out of the country that, according to the folks I met in El Salvador, was still on the books in 1987. According to Wikipedia, while imperceptible in the census, there is now a very small population of Blacks in El Salvador, living mostly in the capital city of San Salvador.

March 22, 1987

Spent time yesterday in a base-Christian community. Their focus is on academic education, particularly for the children, and for the adults, an overtly political education à la Paulo Freire. It's all about literacy and lessons for improving one's condition, for freedom. [And today], it isn't simply a theory anymore.

We also went to a festival to salute Archbishop Oscar Romero. There were drama plays, songs, talks, etc., from 2 pm. til 5 pm. Given the moving and revolutionary speeches, I wondered about orejas, about what might happen to those speaking on their own behalf. Ran into Jose, the Director of Human Rights in El Salvador who works in the U.S. He was in Pullman at the same time as the Salvadoran Caravan last year and it was good to see him again. The network grows....Today we also met Rafael. He's from Venezuela and is in seminary in the Passionate Community. We have those in Dallas and New Jersey. He has one more year in church here and is in charge of the social end of things, working mostly with base-Christian communities. He wants to serve in El Salvador when he's finished: "In Central America, God is being arisen in the pobre (poor)," he says. He also serves as the principal of a kindergarten nearby. It is all about education, from the youngest to the oldest.

March 24, 1987

Heard stories yesterday all day that were heartening and disheartening at the same time. "Prison is the reality in this country." That's from a father whose son had been tortured and killed. As a Salvadoreña said yesterday: "How can I be a guerrilla? I farm all day and take care of my family!" More than anything I'm learning that the Salvadoran and U.S. military are not trying to "win" this war: They are terrorizing the people into submission! But they (the Salvadoran government) is also not trying to lose the war either, otherwise they would lose the U.S. funding. This war is a business! But a young revolutionary woman told me something very insightful: "It is the perception of the need for power. If you appear weak, the world community will perceive you as weak. If you appear strong, if you try to make a life for yourselves and family despite what's being done, you'll be perceived as strong. That's what we are trying to do...."

And she's right. There is a sort of ethos here, a commitment to freedom. The friendly people on the walk yesterday. The family who dished up watermelon (tons of it!) and whom we visited with as we walked. The family whose house had stood with just minor damage from the mortaring and the earthquake, while those across the street crumbled to the ground. The families living in the streets. The family who, on a shoemaker's salary, had Cokes waiting to be served to "Rafael's guests." Then there's Rafael, who is truly a light in this earthquake-ridden communidad, trying to continue educational programs and be a pillar of faith for people to lean on. There are the children in the tin-sided portables because their school had fallen to the ground. The piles, the dust, the potholes, the rebuilding, the sonrisas of the children. It was and is a very heart-wrenching experience. Amongst these pile of rocks and hills, the bombs, and an earthquake, Salvadoreños have managed to build a new community, with hope and vision and faith. There is a strength unyielding. And it just doesn't seem fair that on top of the war and the economic problems, an earthquake shakes their world right to the core. But they seem only to have faltered a bit: They continue to stand.

...We just finished the march for Archbishop Oscar Romero which started at about 9:45 am at La Basilica. It's a stunningly beautiful church. We'd each made crosses this morning out of whatever we could find in the earthquake remnants, to be set in front of the grave of Archbishop Romero at the end of the march.

The procession was huge, about 10,000 people. We marched all the way to the cathedral where Archbishop Rivera y Damas was saying mass. I understand the actual more senior archbishop went on a retreat with several other priests this day, seen as a deliberate slap in the face for the people. No wonder they still hang on to the memories of Archbishop Romero: He was the priest who stood with the people. We saw the folks from Tres Ceibas at the march. It was so good to see the kids and the women: We feel like a family somehow.

But the military reared its ugly head today as well. All along the march were those green uniforms and huge machine guns. A military helicopter just flew over, watching the people and just reminding them who "rules." If only they knew the truth: The PEOPLE are in charge in El Salvador!

I was really moved after mass this morning. There was a group of women whose children, husbands, and relations had been "disappeared" by military forces. They are called "The Mothers of the Disappeared," and they wore white kerchiefs over their heads with CO-MADRES painted in black and black cotton dresses with the same written in white on their backs. I can only imagine how they felt inside—and how my very own mother is feeling right now. But, God willing, I won't be a disappeared person: I'll return to her.

Along the march, the CO-MADRES were singing Nosotros Venceremos (We Shall Overcome) and preaching through bullhorns the words of Dr. Martin Luther King. How powerful a connection this was for me, having sung this song all of my life in English in the U.S. Now, in Spanish, I sing along with my Salvadoran sisters, bearing witness to their losses, our losses. Black people have been influential in changing the world in revolutionary ways. I was very proud to be an African American at that moment. And I realized that words of love are indeed everybody's song.

There was a little baby baptized at the service. She was the daughter of people killed in the war and had been orphaned at San Roque. She was then adopted by Rolando and his wife. They wanted her to be baptized with all of us as the world's godparents of this child. How special it was! A styrofoam cup over a plastic bucket and a smiling loving child, surrounded by her "parents," all of us committed to making the world a better place for her. Her name was Jacqueline Yvonne, an "imported name," says Father Trini, laughing....Indeed.

March 25, 1987

We left this morning for the airport at 6:15 am. The ride there was beautiful (we hadn't seen it on the way in because it was dark). We didn't know if we'd be able to get on the plane because only two of us had reservations that were confirmed. But, we're on it now and heading home.

We got stopped by the police last night. It was more than a little scary but we managed okay. I was glad I was sitting down inside the truck so as not to draw attention, to create a risk for others.... The officers just flashed their lights, checked Rafael's I.D. and let us go. In hindsight, I'm glad we had that experience of fear that people have daily here, as we've heard this is a common practice in El Salvador: This is how people "disappear." Rafael was with us. He just kept saying "Ay, Dios... Ay Dios:" His fear was real: And that was true for all of us in different ways....

March 26, 1987

How do I feel, having spent this time in El Salvador? A whole gamut of feelings come to mind: joy, sorrow, indignation, anger, fear, strength, hope, connectedness to my new Salvadoran friends y mas.... Part of me wanted badly to stay and experience more time in such a beautiful country. Part of me wanted to leave to return to the U.S. to begin the work I know I must do and to keep my hope and my faith as strong as the Salvadoran people's faith. I think, in some ways, that will be the hardest part. We have a long, arduous, tedious task of persuading and teaching people that there are better ways to solve problems than with guns or tanks or taking the lives of thousands of people each year. That the war machine, too often funded by the U.S., is wrong. And now I know, with and by my own experience that people are suffering tremendously as a result. Add a natural catastrophe like the earthquake and the problem is multiplied so greatly.

Probably, the most profound thing experienced on this trip was the warmth and the love of the Salvadoran people. People en el campo, willing to share their food, of which they had little and certainly less variety than some of our poorest of the poor in the U.S. The children rushing to carry your bags to the truck for you. The warm Cokes waiting for you and your sweaty, parched friends after a long walk through earthquake-ridden communities. Invitations with open arms into very simple homes, many barely rebuilt since the earthquake. Trucks and drivers mysteriously appearing to carry the Norte Americanos here and there. Father Trini said it best as we were riding from the convivencia to the Martinezes's for dinner. He said that the Salvadoran people take their faith very seriously. They don't have the luxury of being faithful only when it is convenient or easy: They must be faithful and hopeful every minute of their lives. How difficult that must be, amidst the terror, the fear, the poverty, to take time—make time—to be faithful. The Salvadorans I met taught me powerful lessons of what it means to be in solidarity and true community with others, many of whom I will never ever forget. And it's those lessons that will serve as my religious, spiritual, and moral wisdom and work as I return to the States. And I feel strengthened already. Amen y gracias por todo.

Living Ghana, affirming community: Relationship in practice

Within an *Ubuntu* approach to being in community, I am because you are. So, I want to start this discussion of the importance of Battle's (2009) notion of developing a communal self with one of many experiences that happened while I was on sabbatical, living in Ghana, and writing this book. It involved a man we referred to as Old Soldier. Old Soldier is a retired Ghana military officer who is building his house right next to the new primary school that we are building in Mpeasem. Because we were all working on our projects, there were always stacks of blocks, piles of sea sand, and chipped rocks, all waiting to be put into service as walls or pillars or in creating concrete and sand blocks. While we all were using similar materials, everyone was very clear about whose building supplies belonged to whom.

We developed a very cordial relationship with Old Soldier. He and his wife were very excited about the possibility (and the convenience) of a primary school for their grandchildren right next door to their new house. Just outside their door was a beautiful pile of sea sand, one that we'd purposely bought the previous year so that it would be perfect for plastering (because it's sea sand, you want the rain to take away most of the salt before it's used). One day, we arrived at the site to find half of our sea sand was gone. My husband Henry immediately confronted Old Soldier: Did he take it? Why didn't he call to ask if he could use the sand (which suggested that he was a thief)? Did he not think that we would notice? Old Soldier pleaded his case, begging and asking for forgiveness, as is the case when one has done wrong and needs the other to understand the situation that led to the wrong-doing. As we were leaving (me, not happily, I might add), Old Soldier asked that I forgive him and asked that I also continue to plead on his behalf to my husband. Henry and I talked about this "breach" and our inability to trust Old Soldier now. And for me that meant *forever*.

Several days later, we were back at the school project site. Now very suspicious of Old Soldier, I wanted us to use up ALL of our materials at the site as quickly as possible so that they wouldn't go missing like the sand. I inspected everything on the site that day. I rather curtly greeted Old Soldier, letting him know by my actions that I was still not happy with him. But what struck me was that Henry seemed to have forgotten Old Soldier's transgression, joking and laughing with him as if the sand—OUR sand—was still there on the site! And the next thing I knew, we had 10 much-needed bags of cement (on credit) from Old Soldier, with which to carry on our project.

When I asked Henry about what seemed a shift in his trust of Old Soldier and the "gift" of the cement, he clearly acknowledged and reiterated Old Soldier's wrong-doing in taking our sand. "But maybe he needed it, Cynth," he continued. "We don't know what he's going through. He shares a boundary with us and he's here if we need him in the future. And right now we have what we need, too."

I believe that one of the hardest parts of *Ubuntu* for Africans living in diaspora and in the West is living a communal life, a life that asks us to create and practice individual discipline and habits of living in physical and conscious proximity of others, in community. And when we commit to *Ubuntu* as a living spirituality, we also commit to affirming community as a spiritual mandate, as something that we do that is sacred, that we both (re)member and *refuse* to forget. It is a covenant between us and divine energy that is a fundamental, life-affirming part of our daily existence, that fills us up and pushes us forward to embrace and create the community we need (both within and outside of ourselves) to face the challenges of the world today.

One of those challenges is discovering who we are through others. In the story above, what I thought I "knew" was that Old Soldier seemed greedy and in my mind, dishonest. But what Henry "knew" was that there may have been issues or purposes for his behavior that we might never know. But in the end, maintaining a relationship—that is, being in community—with Old Soldier was more important and what was required. And if my own personhood is discovered through others, dehumanizing Old Soldier (that is, making him "pay" forever for taking our sand) did very little to create the community I desired. The other key? Old Soldier, in Henry's view, was more important than the sand: His personhood in total—as a retired soldier, a husband, a father, a child of God—was what needed to be affirmed, honored, and protected in our relationship with him. That is the sacred nature of *Ubuntu*.

From an African spiritual perspective and an endarkened feminist standpoint, life and spiritual expressions are one and the same, as the sacred is so intimately connected with everyday life. And maintaining the balance of one's individuality with the health and wealth of the community is of value within African culture, both traditionally and contemporarily. However, the challenge for the African ascendant in diaspora who also chooses to (re)member Africa is also a challenge of embracing and living culture that finds space for both African and Western ways of community. Like the story above, living and being in Ghana has provided numerous opportunities to recognize just how much growing up in the West has influenced my understanding of individuality and community, an understanding which often limits my ability to (re)member and to practice community wherever I find myself in the world. This is part of the Western inheritance: A deep sense of value in our unique qualities, individual gifts, and the beauty and talents of our individual selves. In the United States, we physically live in relatively individualistic and independent ways, often making decisions based on our nuclear families, living in our own houses, in different towns than our parents and families, etc. However, in Ghana, I continue to learn the value of communal experience and living "as formative of the person" (Battle, 2009, p. 87): This is my inheritance and the gift of Africa. Learning to live in close proximity with Old Soldier and with consciousness of community is not always easy, but it does enlarge my circle of care, my African family, my sense of responsibility to the larger community. *I am because we are*. I am suggesting that it is the reconciliation of these two values that forms *Ubuntu* for the African in diaspora—and for anyone seeking to be in community with African people on the continent and in the diaspora as well. But it is also the recognition that each part of our identity as African Americans enriches the other, maybe necessarily so. Living *Ubuntu* suggests that we seek contexts, people, and practices on both sides of the water that do not require that we separate our personhood as African ascendants: Ourselves from our spirits, our knowledges from their communities of origin, our histories from their diverse roots and memories, our various identities one from the other. Practicing a communal self requires us to bring all of that energy into the room wherever we find ourselves on the globe.

A postscript: Pedagogies in the spirit of community

Embracing a commitment to the spirit of *Ubuntu* quite naturally may lead you to engagements in the world and to a deepened spirituality through them. I've shared here some of the most striking cultural memories for me, moments in time that continue to make a demand on my present being as a teacher and a researcher. Such memories of living community can serve as a point of reference, a touchstone for our behavior and for making sense of the world (Strong-Wilson, 2008). But while I am continually asked by teachers to prescribe a model or a precise *Ubuntu* pedagogy, here too, I will resist: There is no simple nor should there be a singular model for being, developing, or creating community. As Fernandes (2003) states: "to suggest otherwise is to mistake spiritual learning for ownership or missionary activity" (p. 117). The profundity of embracing a commitment to *Ubuntu* is in the way that a such a commitment changes your very personhood to one that sees, feels, deeply respects, and is responsible for the inner being that you are and the inter-being that you need: I am because you are. I lean again on Fernandes (2003):

> It is a process which brings you face to face with the boundedness of time, space, and history. It is a process that demands an unimaginable intensity of labor in an endeavor which will always seem unfinished....It is the essence of the unrepresentable, which Western postmodern intellectuals have been paralyzed by only because they have mistaken the unrepresentable for the unrealizable. It is the only form of power, that lived divinity, that can transform and transcend all forms of hierarchy, injustice and repression. (p. 118)

In all my wanderings in this world, what has been most interesting as an African ascendant person is exploring and feeling the ways that people all over the world—including many whom I teach—embody a similar life manner and faithfulness that also exists in African ascendant communities today. A complex and supportive sense of extended family. A sense of harmony with nature. A faith in the invisible world of the spirits alive in the visible, and the lack of separation between the spiritual and the material in everyday life. As teachers, we must recognize that inviting the particular and communal memory of Africans and others marginalized in our societies into experience of community is what will make the spiritual experience intelligible and useful to us all. And part of the power of our cultural memory is in what it leaves behind spiritually and emotionally for others, what "propels the memory into a living, breathing, everyday consciousness that, even [with time], cannot be quieted" (Rodriguez & Fortier, 2007). For the African ascendant in diaspora, W.E.B. Du Bois (1989) spoke of these emotional whispers of memory as our spiritual strivings, as our ongoing desire and quest to bring a sense of clarity to what he described as both our African and American souls. Articulated as a question: "As I face Africa, I ask myself: What is it between us that constitutes a tie that I can feel better than I can explain" (Du Bois, 1986, pp. 639-670)? This is not a frivolous question in the work of (re)membering culture. Soyinka (1999) puts the gravity of the question in this way: "What is Africa to me? This was a question that inspired more than mere poetry or rhetoric—it informed, in one way or another, the socio-political existence of many" (p. 145). And this is the power of embracing *Ubuntu* in teaching and learning: It encourages us to expand, to draw the boundaries of community beyond our selves for the purpose of deepening our understanding at the level of cosmology, of the very way that peoples and societies imagine and structure themselves. Choosing to be in community is a spiritual striving: Being drawn into community in ways that transform the core of our existence as African ascendants is our work. In that space of spiritual community, we can see the very essence of our existence and survival as human beings as interdependent, interrelated and connected. Choosing to embrace and practice *Ubuntu* also becomes a space where we might recognize African cosmology not simply being applicable to those of African heritage but as a way for the world to recover and (re)member "spiritual insight about how we are all related to each other and to creation" (Battle, 2009, p. 87). Such a choice, in teaching and research would, in my eyes, be revolutionary. However, choosing options that privilege the economically poor, the marginalized, and the oppressed and being transformed in community together is also a space of liberatory pedagogy for the privileged. And in the spirit of *Ubuntu*, neither the privileged and the poor have reached the time to rest. Instead it is time to be responsible for the energy we bring to the communities we create. I end here with a meditation in tribute to the spirit of *Ubuntu*.

Resting

How can I rest,
As an African woman of the world,
When the world so close around me
Is working so hard?
This is the question
I ask myself every day here in Ghana:
How can I rest?

How can I rest
When request after request
Touches my heart so deeply.
"Madam, please can you help me?"
I want to weep—and do so often.

How can I rest
As I look out from my modest but cozy
Air-conditioned room,
To the village outside my window
And see school-aged children
Who've never stepped foot
Inside a school?

How can I rest
When the call to wake each morning
Is the sound of a man with a machete
Cutting the grass or
The swish, swish of a broom,
A sister readying the home for the day?

How can I rest
When I know
That the young man who cleans my room each day
Earns for his six-day work week about
$15 per month, from which
he has expenses to pay each month just like I do?

How can I rest
When I know that part of the reason
For the struggle of my Ghanaian brothers and sisters

Is intimately tied to the economic hardship and
Material desire created by the likes of CNN,
And perpetrated by the country in which I have an address?

How can I rest
As one of many sisters passes me on the street,
Balancing a heavy aluminum pan
Full of fish
On her head,
A child tied to her back,
And another one holding her hand?

And it is this very sister, Lord
Her back so straight,
Her strength so apparent,
That You have sent
As the answer to my question.

I can rest in knowing that in every situation,
I too can find balance.
I can rest because I know
That I am not
my sister or brother's keeper,
I am my sister or brother,
Each of us responsible,
Not for the circumstances that created
The particularity of our hardships (or lack their of),
But for what we do with those circumstances,
Your gifts.
I can rest in identifying,
not begrudgingly
But joyously,
with those who are suffering around me.
I can rest in the love
That is the wave of the sister's hand,
That is the sister's smile from under the pan on her head.
I can rest in the love
Of a life of service,
And gratitude for the divinity of Your hand,
Knowing that each soul
Will have to give its own account
For *itself*.

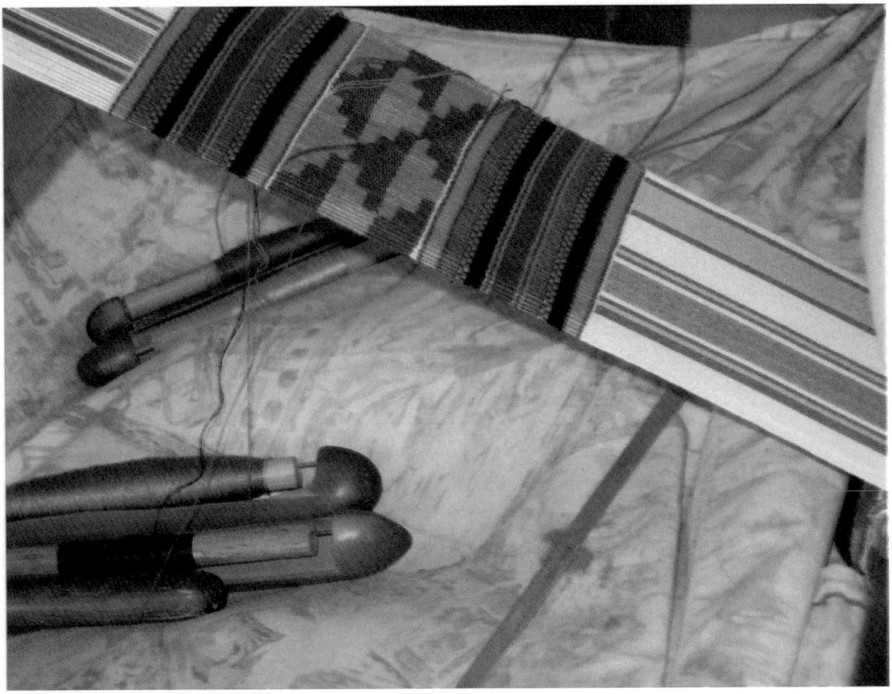

CHAPTER SEVEN

The Ability to Create Anew

(Re)membering to Make the World We Want

> One of the first things the despot Duvalier tried to take away from them was the mythic element of their stories…Aime Cesaire, Frantz Fanon, or Albert Camus.…Unlike the country's own citizens, these writers could neither be tortured or murdered themselves nor cause their family members to be tortured or murdered. And no matter how hard he tried, Pap Doc Duvalier *could not make their words go away.* Their maxims and phrases would keep coming back, buried deep in memories by the rote recitation techniques that the Haitian school system had taught so well. (Danticat, 2010, p. 9, emphasis mine)

I find inspiration in these words, written by an amazingly insightful and award-winning Haitian woman writer, Edwidge Danticat. The title of her recent book is itself a provocation to all who call ourselves teachers: *Create Dangerously: The Immigrant Artist at Work* (2010). In this text, she shares how the work of reading, writing, and (re)membering (on which teaching and research rely) are always dangerous undertakings. She speaks to how the work of an intellectual is the work of an artist, of creating the world through one's words, one's art, one's life. Particular to the work of education, her call is one that incites us to look both forward and backward, engaging our cultural memories to produce new spaces in which we all might live more fully. For me, it is also a call to recognize our roles as teachers and researchers as serious life-or-death endeavors: Each encounter with ideas, each class we teach, each research study we undertake is imbued with the possibility of creation, of making something new and different, an outcome that may create something even better and more just than what already exists. It is a mandate to create the texts that don't just sit on the shelves in our offices or that are worshiped by colleagues, reified in our scholarly journals. I am suggesting here that what we might instead create are the texts that have the same potential as art, that can actually inspire, literally breathing new life into the work of another.

> Create dangerously, for people who read dangerously…knowing in part that no matter how trivial your words may seem, someday, somewhere, someone may risk his or her life to read them…somewhere, if not now…[as writers, teachers] we may also save someone's life. (Danticat, 2010, p. 10)

This has been the legacy of the African experience, captured and shared in the work of our artists, painters, musicians, and writers of literature and poetry. For many of these artists, the work of creating art is a very explicit embrace of the responsibility to (re)member Africa and her diaspora. Their call as artists is a concomitant call to activism, activism designed primarily to help us know and (re)member ourselves as African ascendant people. But as Danticat (2010) further suggests, the call to activism is to also see our work as that which, right now or in the future, might literally *save* the life of another. It reminds me of those artists of life who, gratefully, have truly been my lifesavers and touchstones as an African ascendant woman scholar. Where would my teaching and research be without bell hooks, Patricia Hill Collins, Abena Busia, and Gloria Anzaldúa? Without Frantz Fanon, Paulo Freire, Ayi Kwei Armah, or W.E.B. Du Bois? Without Alice Walker, Toni Morrison, James Baldwin, or Paule Marshall? Without Elizabeth Catlett, Jacob Lawrence, Frida Kahlo, and Edna Kwame? Without Maya Angelou, Margaret Walker, Langston Hughes, and Sonia Sanchez? Without Dianne Reeves, Jonathan Butler, Bob Marley, and Mahalia Jackson? Without Martin Luther King Jr., Thich Nhat Hanh, Iyanla Vanzant, and Pastor Incoom? My point in this very incomplete but powerful roll call is that our work of teaching and research must also be work of (re)membering for the purpose of *creating* the world that we want, of (re)membering African wisdom and culture as our activism in the spirit and remembrance of our artists. One thing that is true of those listed above (and of the many thousands of African artists not mentioned) is that the process of creating art that tells the truth also requires courage, faith, and understanding of the greater good, as these artists too often risked everything including their lives, to (re)member who we are as a people. It is through their (re)membering and the choice to create what was necessary for our survival as a people that a way has been opened for those of us who chose to (re)member the gifts they have given us.

This may be one of the reasons many African ascendants in diaspora are drawn to Africa, drawn to develop intimate and creative relationships there. In our various migrations, the intentional movements back and forth, the settling ins and temporary leavings, we engage in our own sort of creative globalization, one that fills in the blanks of our African history and cultural memory and opens spaces for new productions of African culture as we (re)member. And in the words that we write, teach, and create in publications like this one, I am suggesting that we might also focus our attention not just on the nature of these migrations to and from Africa but on what others can do with what we have produced from those migratory experiences. This is Hall's (1999) thesis, that is, that the unity and creativity of Africa and her diaspora lie not in "recovering" some mystical or mythical Africa but in the ways that engagements with African people, knowledge, and wisdom produce and create new versions and visions of African culture. This engagement is embodied in Anzaldúa's call to a spiritual activism, designed to work against the convenience of binaries, to marshal inclusivity, and to address the needs of our global and multicultural twenty first century (Keating, 2008). It is embedded in Danticat's (2010) call that we "create dangerously, as though each piece of art were a stand-in for a life, a soul, a future...*we have no other choice*" (p. 20, emphasis mine). Learning to (re)member the things we've learned to forget is to also recognize in cultural memories the work of the spiritual, the energy that enables us to create something new, different, necessary. That is the work of a spiritual activism that (re)members.

To be like water: An open letter to my colleagues, with love, from Ghana

---

February 2008

To my dear friends & colleagues,

This letter (or I should say the thinking and reflection that has led to it), has not been easy.... The landscapes of my mind and heart have been filled with so many memories, musings, and desires. What I really wish is that this conversation were happening right here in Ghana, face to face, with the ocean (and a few Star beers) as our inspiration.

I have just finished a book by Charlie Ryrie and David Cavagnaro (1999) called the *Healing Energies of Water,* in preparation for a retreat focused on the sacred waters of Ghana and a rather personal interest in my watery Scorpio nature. I am also reading Barack Obama's (2004) *Dreams from My Father*, which is a stunning memoir centered on race and its complexities and meanings, made even more poignant as we followed his incredible journey to the presidency from here in Ghana. And today, it feels so good to be cheering for a brother, a living thinker, a comrade in the struggles for equality, dignity, social justice, and change. And the people of Ghana are cheering too, our "son of Africa" as he is affectionately referred to here. I have also just finished Dalton's (1996) *Racial Healing: Confronting the Fear between Blacks and Whites*. And although I find his analysis of the dynamics and history of race far too simplistic, full of contradictions, and rather sexist in nature, there is one notion he raises worth mentioning: That conversations about identity and culture are based both in memory and in the humanity that we are living those memories right now. And for Black folks in particular, we have to begin to "rethink and retell who we are and how racism [and race] have affected our lives" (Dalton, 1996, p. 9).

And I am struck by the connections that have come to me between the spiritual nature of water and the meanings of Black identity for African people in our varying versions. Ryrie and Cavagnaro (1999) talk about water in spiritual as well as creative terms:

> Water has no form but gives form to everything. It is billions of years old, but can constantly rejuvenate itself. It provides a constant interchange between the Earth and the cosmos. Every drop is a microcosm of the universe, carrying information from ancient eras and from worlds we cannot understand. (p. 13)

In other words, water (re)members all of life: It is present life, the seeds of future life, and the memory of past life. Water has a memory based on what it has experienced or what cycles it has gone through. So its health and thus our consequent health depend on how we care for its experiences. And this is also the story of African people: Ancient, life affirming, giving meaning to people far beyond ourselves. The authors go on to talk about how there are different types of water, some more healthy than others. And I was struck by the definition and description of distilled water or what scientists refer to as "pure water":

> It is not found anywhere in nature and it contains no dissolved materials....Its purity means that it grasps at everything within reach, seeking to absorb minerals and nutrients wherever it finds them. (p. 89)

That sort of grasping is what I believe have been the efforts, over the past 400+ years for African Americans, as we continue to work to make sense of ourselves, our "deep" cultures and histories beginning long before arriving on Western shores. It also describes our responses to the racism inherent in the American experiment. But the next part just blew me away, as I thought about the impact that such grasping has had on our very selves, on the spirit of Black folks, and our ability to create:

> Distilled water is sometimes classified as immature water, lacking those subtle energies that convey and impart health: It has no history, no memory of glacial waters or rocky pools, fast flowing currents or meandering channels, earth minerals, sunshine, or shady places, or any other influences that affect the health of the water. (p. 89)

Let's be clear. I am not suggesting that Black people are immature or have no history or memory: Quite the contrary. For me this passage rather describes the fluid nature, the ever-changing landscape of life for Black people—and the possibilities that exist in experiencing and engaging *African* cultural heritage and knowledges. As I sit here in

Ghana, an ascendant of her shores (that is, of Africa) and of the shores of the United States, I draw much inspiration from traveling back (and forth) to this place of deep memory, culture, and tradition. And this quest to become full of ourselves as Black people is really about becoming more "mature," about deepening our understandings of who we really are as African ascendants by wrestling and wandering within and through the past and seeing its traces on our lives today. Barack Obama reminds me of this Truth, as he quotes Faulkner's notion of history as really "never dead and buried—it isn't even past. This collective history, this past, directly touches my own" (p. x).

That makes being here in Ghana also a place of great challenge in the revisiting, in the (re)membering. It is the work of deepening one's consciousness of Africa by not trying to marshal a fixed understanding of what is "African," but instead living with/in one that is fluid, productive, *creative*. That is how so many Black people in the diaspora who may never have traveled to Africa can be so deeply influenced by it. It's about consciousness of the cultural memories of Africa that follow you wherever you are. Like water, they are collective ever-changing memories that flow, the "river where blood is born" (Jackson-Opoku, 1999). Here in Ghana, it's also an attempt to fill in the memory of the "fast flowing currents and meandering channels" mentioned above that are sometimes painful and confusing but necessary prerequisites to naming the pain in order to transform it. It's about going shopping for new toilets for our house in Ghana and having the prices nearly tripled after the shop owner saw me in the van and assumed that I have unlimited amounts of money at my disposal. It's about my own ill-feelings and very harsh judgments when I see a 60+-year-old White man with a big belly gallivanting on the beach with a 20+-year-old Ghanaian woman, their baby son oblivious to the harsh stares not just from me but from others. It's in the very clipped greeting I gave to some White folks from the U.S. on a Christian missionary trip to Ghana who wanted me to serve as their cultural interpreter, asking a whole lot of questions about why I am in Ghana, the people I know who might be of service to them, and how I negotiate and "deal with the local Ghanaians." It's in my immediate desire to cuss them out. It's in the jumble of emotions (joy? guilt? heartache?) I have each time we go to the new school site to pay the guys who are working there and how thrilled they are to receive the 12 Ghana *cedis* (about US$8) for their day's labor in the hot sun, especially given that the minimum wage is between $3 and $4.00 a day. I could go on. But the joy of being here in Ghana is the space and energy to reflect, to rethink, and to heal. To come to a sort of reconciliation in life of one's burdens and privileges, one's identity(ies) and opportunities as a citizen of the U.S. and of the world. It gives me a context (and time, precious time…) to be more conscious and present to the ways I see myself, am seen (or not) by others, and how I relate to the world around me. I think these meanderings have been important in finding a way to let go (if only temporarily) of the constant and continuous anger and hostility about the ways that race, as a social contract, has truly deprived us all of our humanity. And, like the water, I am very interested in health: Of the planet, of Black people, of the world, of the way we naturally gravitate *towards* each other. Here in Ghana, finding ways toward each other as African ascendants both affirms and deepens personhood, arising from the deep well of memories of what kinship and community might be. However painful, tentative, and hard, learning to be because we all are is the way forward.

Just as I was trying to finish this letter on the hotel computer, a very demanding White woman with a pin-drive in her hand came up to me. She wanted to let me know that she "needed this computer," demanding to know "when I'd be finished" and that I "really had to let her use it now." I responded to her rudeness by calmly letting her know that I was also a guest in the hotel, and she would have to wait until I was finished doing my work. And given the way she approached me, I have a feeling that her demanding sense of White (female) privilege is also her everyday way of being, seeing Black folks as existing solely to serve her needs. For her, it's about her rights as a White woman to demand and the need for others to respond. But not today. The good news? During her tantrum, another White couple walked into the lobby, along with their two children. And the minute the smaller son saw me sitting at the computer, he immediately started smiling and walking (more like running!) toward me. Having reached the place where I sat, he tentatively walked along the front of the desk, placing his little hands one right after the other until he'd come around the the desk, right by my side. I looked up and smiled at him, thrilled that he wasn't afraid of me (as so many White children I meet here are). "Hi," I said cheerfully. By now, just a couple feet away from me, he smiled, waved and said "Hi!" His joy both surprised and delighted me. Not missing a beat, he said, "I like computers, too!" And just as quickly, he turned and ran back to his folks, waving at me as he left the building. His presence made me happy and put the whirlwind White woman before him in proper perspective: The lessons we can learn about joy, respect, and spirit from children of the world are profound.

Love and blessings from Ghana,
Cynthia

Truth: (Re)membering the capital "T"

The Truth shall set you free? Maybe. But first the Truth must be set free. (Soyinka, 1999, p. 13, emphasis his)

This book has been a labor of love, one of trying to articulate some of the lessons that African ascendant people—and those who care about their own humanity—might explore, lift up, (re)member. And Keating (2008) points the way through Gloria Anzaldúa's idea of spiritual activism, to the sort of praxis that begins when there is a shift or transformation in one's inner self that simultaneously influences one's outer or public acts. But as we have explored some of the lessons we need to (re)member as Black people, I turn our attention toward the idea of Truth (with a capital T), as articulated by Soyinka. What is the core of our Truth, as African ascendant people, that which is unmovable, unshakable, always already within us, that Truth that I've sought to set free in these pages? Probably the most important is this: That our spiritual being as African ascendant people generally and women particularly is a powerful space from which to examine and create fuller visions and versions of ourselves as Black people. But how does (re)membering bring us into the realm where spirituality is a bridge, a space where we are a part of the creative community that we seek? I believe as Anzaldúa and others do that (re)membering spirit pushes us to create such bridges backward *and* forward, through memories and experiences of places and people that we have forgotten, including ourselves.

I find myself reminded here of Asa Hilliard (Nana Baffour Amankwatia II), the tremendous brother-scholar and Ghanaian king to whom many of us, as African ascendant scholars, owe a great deal of gratitude. It was his scholarship and voice that opened the way for us to explore more deeply the lessons of African identity and culture that I have humbly attempted to raise up in this book. I (re)member being at a talk he gave at the 2000 Annual Meeting of the American Educational Research Association (AERA), one where he specifically addressed his remarks directly to African American scholars. But this was not a praisesong. He chastised us for continuing to conduct research for research sake or to amass lines on our vitas. Instead, he argued, we needed to engage research on the bigger questions of both the quality of services and the distribution of those services to Black children. He stressed that our work as African ascendant scholars was not to do more studies on poverty in Black communities or to continue to speak of Black families in pathological terms. His point was rather an epistemological and political one, that is, that we must begin our research, teaching, and our very lives from the premise that we—and our children—are brilliant and capable and that, if all things are "equal," Black children will perform equally as well or better than their White counterparts. Our focus as Black scholars, he suggested needed to be on creating and fostering qualities in Black communities and schools using African frameworks and perspectives (and implicitly, cultural memories) as the bases of our analysis. And embedded in Nana's call for quality was also a call to create and foster our spiritual activism as well, to be reminded of the profound legacy of African people as the ground from which we do our work as teachers and researchers.

In the tradition of our African kings and queens, Nana unapologetically and directly spoke to our Black community on that day. He reminded us of the spiritual and cultural mandate we have to educate all African ascendant children. Among his many points raised that day, he (re)minded us that African American people, as a cultural group, are unconscious in a global sense as African people. He stated that we have "acute amnesia" as a group and a dire need to (re)member the cultural memories and knowledge that we as a people have created. And while Nana's indictment was a stinging one, its truth is unquestionable. As Africans, we are the ones who can create the world that we want for our children, the ones who must situate our lives and the work of education in the long memory, culture, and traditions of African people. We must, as I have attempted to do here, examine the connections between the African continent and the diaspora for our knowledges and our cultural imperatives, for the meanings of who we've been, are, and might be in/to the world. The continent of Africa and her individual countries like Ghana are critical and fruitful sites for developing the consciousness that enables us to not only transform ourselves but to transform the conditions of African people—and thus all people—in the world. Regardless of the contexts within which we choose to create ourselves and our conditions anew as African people, the call here is to *consciously* do so. And memory and history must be both our sites of resistance and of creation, as knowledge of the stories of African peoples is knowledge of the very history and humanity of all…

> Memory like art reminds us that eventually it is the "event" that becomes something to remember. But we can't capture it: We can only remember it.
>
> This is what I've always seen as the unifying principle among all writers [artists]. This is what, among other things, might join Albert Camus and Sophocles to Toni Morrison, Alice Walker, Osip Mandelstam, and Ralph Waldo Emerson to Ralph Waldo Ellison….They have given us a passport, making us honorary citizens of their culture. (Danticat, 2010, p. 10)

As we "make peace between what has happened to [us], what the world is, and what it should be" (Anzaldúa, 1981, p. 208), we must (re)member ourselves in order to create the world that does not yet exist for African ascendant people. We have the lessons and legacy of artists of life like Nana Baffour Amankwatia II among others, the gifts of cultural memories that we need to create the world that we want. And in the spirit of our teachers, our artists, and the ancestors, that is a space of creativity and spiritual activism worth (re)membering. Let it be so.

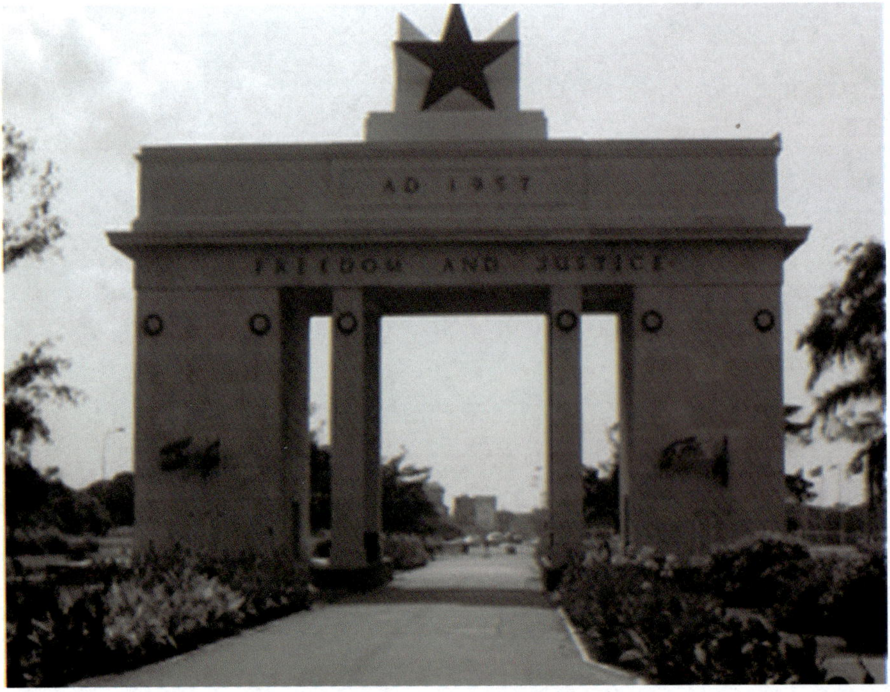
AD 1957
FREEDOM AND JUSTICE

REFERENCES

Aidoo, A. A. (1970). *No sweetness here and other stories.* Harlow, UK: Longman.

Aidoo, A.A. (1998). The African woman today. In O. Nnaemeka (Ed.) *Sisterhood: Feminisms and power from Africa to the diaspora.* Trenton, NJ: African World Press.

Aina, O. (1998). African women at the grassroots. In O. Nnaemeka (Ed.), *Sisterhood: Feminisms and power from Africa to the diaspora.* Trenton, NJ: Africa World Press.

Akyeampong, E. & Obeng, P. (2005). Spirituality, gender and power in Asante history. In O. Oyewumi (Ed.), *African gender studies: A reader.* New York: Palgrave.

Alexander, M. J. (2005). *Pedagogies of crossing: Meditations on feminism, sexual politics, memory, and the sacred.* Durham, NC: Duke University Press.

Amadiume, I. (1987). *Male daughters, female husbands: Gender and sex in an African society.* London: Zed Books.

American Heritage Dictionary of the English Language (2000). Boston: Delta Books.

Angelou, M. (1990). *I shall not be moved.* New York: Random House.

Ani, M. (1994). *Yurugu: An African-centered critique of European cultural thought and behavior.* Trenton, NJ: Africa World Press.

Anzaldúa, G. (1981). La prieta. In C. Moraga & G. Anzaldúa (1983) *This bridge called my back: Writings by radical women of color.* New York: Kitchen Table/Women of Color Press.

Anzaldúa, G. (1999). *Borderlands/La frontera: The new Mestiza.* San Francisco: Aunt Lute.

Appiah, K.A. (1992). *In my father's house: Africa in the philosophy of culture.* New York: Oxford University Press.

Appiah, K. A. (2006). *Cosmopolitanism: Ethics in a world of strangers.* New York: W.W. Norton.

Arie. India. (2006). I choose. On *Testimony, Volume 1: Life and relationships* [CD]. Detroit: Motown. (Release date 2/08/2007)

Aristizabal, H. & Lefer, D. (2010). *The blessing is next to the wound: A story of art, activism, and transformation.* Brooklyn, NY: Lantern Books.

Armah, A.K. (1973). *Two thousand seasons.* Oxford, England: Heinemann.

Bambara, T.C. (1970). *The Black woman: An anthology.* New York: New American Library.

Bambara, T.C. (1980/1992). *The salt eaters.* New York: Random House.

Bargna, I. (2000). *African art.* Milan, Italy: Jaca Book.

Battle, M. (2009). *Ubuntu: I in you and you in me.* New York: Seabury Books.

Behar, R. (1996). *The vulnerable observer: Anthropology that breaks your heart.* Boston: Beacon.

Bell-Scott, P. (1994). *Life notes: Personal writings by contemporary Black women.* New York: W.W. Norton.

Bethel, L. (1982). "This infinity of conscious pain": Zora Neale Hurston and the Black female literary tradition. In G. T. Hull, P.B. Scott, & B. Smith (Eds.), *All the women are White, all the Blacks are men, but some of us are brave.* New York: The Feminist Press.

Booth, W. J. (2006). *Communities of memory: On witness, identity, and justice.* Ithaca, NY: Cornell University Press.

Brah, A. (1999). The scent of memory: Strangers, our own, and others. *Feminist Review*, 61: 4–26.

Brand, D. (2001). *A map to the door of no return: Notes to belonging.* Toronto: Vintage Canada.

Bray, Y.A. (2008). All the 'Africans' are male, all the 'sistas' are 'American,' but some of us resist: Realizing African feminism(s) as an Afrological research methodology. *The Journal of Pan African Studies*, 2(2): 58–73.

Busia, A. (1989). What is your nation? Reconnecting Africa and her diaspora through Paule Marshall's Praisesong for the widow. In C. Wall, (Ed.), *Changing our own words: Essays on criticism, theory, and writing by Black women.* New Brunswick, NJ: Rutgers University Press.

Busia, A. P. A. (1993). Languages of the self. In S.M. James & A.P.A. Busia (Eds.), *Theorizing Black feminisms: The visionary pragmatism of Black women.* London: Routledge.

Butler, J. (1993). *Bodies that matter: On the discursive limits of sex.* New York: Routledge.

Byrd, A.D. & Tharps, L. I. (2001). *Hair story: Untangling the roots of Black hair in America.* New York: St. Martin's Press.

Cannella, G.S. & Manuelito, K.D. (2008). Feminisms from unthought locations: Indigenous worldviews, marginalized feminisms, and revisioning an anticolonial social science. In N. K. Denzin, Y. S. Lincoln, & L. Tuhiwai Smith (Eds.) *Handbook of critical and indigenous methodologies.* Los Angeles: Sage.

REFERENCES

Christian, B. (1985). Ritualistic process and the structure of Paule Marshall's Praisesong for the widow. *Black feminist criticism: Perspectives on Black women writers*. New York: Pergamon.

Cleage, P. (2005). *We speak your names: A celebration*. New York: Random House.

Collins, P.H. (1990). *Black feminist thought: Knowledge, consciousness, and the politics of empowerment*. New York: Routledge.

Collins, P.H. (2000). *Black feminist thought: Knowledge, consciousness, and the politics of empowerment (Second Edition)*. New York: Routledge.

Coloma, R. (2008). Border crossing subjectivities and research: Through the prism of feminists of color. *Race, Ethnicity and Education*, 11, 1: 11–28.

Combahee River Collective (1982). A Black feminist statement. In G.T. Hull, P.B. Scott, & B. Smith (Eds.) *All the women are White, all the Blacks are men, but some of us are brave: Black women's studies*. New York: The Feminist Press.

Cone, J. (1990). *A Black theology of liberation: Twentieth anniversary with critical responses*. Maryknoll, NY: Orbis.

Cooper, A.J. (1892). *A voice from the South: By a woman from the South*. Xenia, OH: The Aldine Printing House.

Couser, G.T. (1996). Oppression and repression: Personal and collective memory in Paule Marshall's *Praisesong for the widow* and Leslie Marmon Silko's *Ceremony*. In A. Singh, J.T. Skerrett, & R.E. Hogan (Eds.) *Memory and cultural politics: New approaches to American ethnic literatures*. Lebanon, NH: Northeastern University Press.

Dalton, H. (1996). *Racial healing: Confronting the fear between Blacks and Whites*. New York: Knopf Doubleday.

Danticat, E. (2010). *Create dangerously: The immigrant artist at work*. Princeton, NJ: Princeton University Press.

Darder, A. (2009). Decolonizing the flesh: The body, pedagogy, & inequality. In R. S. Colinos (Ed.) *The postcolonial challenge of education*. New York: Routledge.

Dash, J. (Producer/Director). (1991). *Daughters of the dust* [Motion picture]. United States: Geechee Girls Productions.

Daza, S. (2008). Decolonizing researcher authenticity. *Race, Ethnicity and Education*, 11, 1: 71–86.

Dei, G. J. S. (2000). Rethinking the role of Indigenous knowledge in the academy. *Journal of Inclusive Education*, 4, 2: 111–132.

Dei, G. J. S. (Ed.). (2011). *Indigenous philosophies and critical education: A reader*. New York: Peter Lang.

Denzin, N. K., Lincoln, Y. S., & Tuhiwai Smith, L. (Eds.), (2008). *Handbook of critical and indigenous methodologies*. Los Angeles: Sage.

Dillard, C. B. (1994). Beyond supply and demand: Critical pedagogy, ethnicity, and empowerment in recruiting teachers of color. *Journal of Teacher Education*, 45: 1–9.

Dillard, C. B. (1996). From lessons of self to lessons of others: Exploring creative autobiography in multicultural learning and teaching. *Multicultural Education,* 4, 2: 33–37.

Dillard, C. B. (2000). The substance of things hoped for, the evidence of things not seen: Examining an endarkened feminist epistemology in educational research and leadership. *The International Journal of Qualitative Studies in Education*, 13: 661–681.

Dillard, C. B. (2003). Cut to heal, not to bleed: A response to Handel Wright's An endarkened feminist epistemology? Identity, difference, and the politics of representation in educational research. *International Journal of Qualitative Studies in Education,* 16(2): 227–232.

Dillard, C. B. (2006a). *On spiritual strivings: Transforming an African American woman's academic life*. Albany: State University of New York Press.

Dillard, C. B. (2006b). When the music changes, so should the dance: Cultural and spiritual considerations in paradigm "proliferation." *International Journal of Qualitative Studies in Education,* 19, 1: 59–76.

Dillard, C. B. (2008). When the ground is Black, the ground is fertile: Exploring endarkened feminist epistemology and healing methodologies of the spirit. In N. Denzin, Y.S. Lincoln, & L. Tuhiwai-Smith (Eds.), *Handbook of critical and indigenous methodologies*. Thousand Oaks, CA: Sage.

Dillard, C. B. (2009). Racializing ethics and bearing witness to memory in research. In N. Denzin & M. Giardina (Eds.), *Qualitative inquiry and social justice*. Walnut Creek, CA: Left Coast Press.

Dillard, C. B. & Bell, C. (2011). Endarkened feminism and sacred praxis: Troubling (auto)ethnography through critical engagements with African indigenous knowledges. In G. Dei (Ed.), *Indigenous philosophies and critical education: A reader*. New York: Peter Lang.

REFERENCES

Dillard, C. B. & Dixson, A. D. (2006). Affirming the will and the way of the ancestors: Black feminist consciousness and the search for good[ness] in qualitative science. In N. Denzin & M. Giardina (Eds.), *Qualitative inquiry and the conservative challenge*. Walnut Creek, CA: Left Coast Press.

Dillard, C. B. & Okpalaoka, C. L. (2011). The sacred and spiritual nature of endarkened transnational feminist praxis in qualitative research. In N. Denzin & Y. S. Lincoln (Eds.), *Handbook of qualitative research (Fourth Edition)*. Thousand Oaks, CA: Sage.

Dillard, C. B., Tyson, C. A., & Abdur-Rashid, D. (2000). My soul is a witness: Affirming pedagogies of the spirit. *International Journal of Qualitative Studies in Education*, 13: 447–462.

Du Bois, W. E. B. (1903/1989). *The souls of Black folk*. New York: Bantam.

DuBois, W. E. B. (1940/2005). *Dusk of dawn: An essay toward an autobiography of a race concept*. New Brunswick, NJ: Transaction Publishers.

Fanon, F. (1967). *Black skin, white masks* (p. 109). London: Pluto Books.

Feelings, T. (1995). *The Middle Passage*. New York: Dial Books.

Fernandes, L. (2003). *Transforming feminist practice: Non-violence, social justice and the possibilities of a spiritualized feminism*. San Francisco: Aunt Lute Books.

Freire, P. (1970). *Pedagogy of the oppressed*. New York: Continuum.

Gilroy, P. (1993). *The Black Atlantic: Modernity and double consciousness*. New York: Verso.

Gutierrez, G. (2003). *We drink from our own wells: The spiritual journey of a people*. Maryknoll, NY: Orbis.

Guy-Sheftall, B. (1995). *Words of fire: An anthology of African-American feminist thought*. New York: The New Press.

Halbwachs, M. (1926/1950). *The collective memory*, translators F. J. & V.Y. Ditter. London: Harper Books.

Hall, S. (1999). Thinking the diaspora: Home-thoughts from abroad. *Small Axe*, 6: 1–18.

Hanh, T. N. (1998). *Teachings on love*. Berkeley, CA: Parallax Press.

Hanh, T. N. (1999). *Call me by my true names: The collected poems of Thich Nhat Hanh*. Berkeley, CA: Parallax Press.

Hilliard, A.G. (1995). *The maroon within us: Selected essays on African American community socialization*. Baltimore: Black Classic Press.

hooks, b. (1981). *Ain't I a woman? Black women and feminism.* Cambridge, MA: South End Press.

hooks, b. (1989). *Talking back: Thinking feminist, thinking black.* Boston: South End Press.

hooks, b. (1992). *Black looks: Race and representation.* Boston: South End Press.

hooks, b. (1993). *Sisters of the yam: Black women and self-recovery.* Cambridge, MA: South End Press

hooks, b. (1994). *Teaching to transgress.* New York: Routledge.

hooks, b. (1999). *Remembered rapture: The writer at work.* New York: Henry Holt.

hooks, b. (2000). *All about love: New visions.* New York: William Morrow.

hooks, b. (2008). *Belonging: A culture of place.* New York: Routledge.

hooks, b. & Mesa-Bains, A. (2006). *Homegrown: Engaged cultural criticism.* Cambridge, MA: South End Press.

hooks, b. & West, C. (1991) *Breaking bread: Insurgent Black intellectual life.* Cambridge, MA: South End Press.

Hudson-Weems, C. (1995). *Africana womanism: Reclaiming ourselves.* Troy, MI: Bedford Publishers.

Hudson-Weems, C. (1998a). Africana womanism. In O. Nnaemeka (Ed.), *Sisterhood: Feminisms and power from Africa to the diaspora.* Trenton, NJ: African World Press.

Hudson-Weems, C. (1998b). Self naming and self definition: An agenda for survival. In In O. Nnaemeka (Ed.), *Sisterhood: Feminisms and power from Africa to the diaspora* (pp. 449–452). Trenton, NJ: African World Press.

Hull, A.G. (2001). *Soul talk: The new spirituality of African American women.* Rochester, VT: Inner Traditions.

Hull, G.T., Bell-Scott, P., & Smith, B. (1982). *All the women are White, all the Blacks are men, but some of us are brave: Black women's studies.* New York: The Feminist Press.

Hurston, Z. N. (1978). *Their eyes were watching God.* Urbana: University of Illinois Press.

Hurtado, A. (2003). Theory in the flesh: Toward an endarkened epistemology. *International Journal of Qualitative Studies in Education,* 16, 2: 215–225.

Husband, T. (2007). Always Black, always male: Race/cultural recollections and the qualitative researcher. Unpublished paper presented at The Congress of Qualitative Inquiry, May 3–6, University of Illinois, Champaign-Urbana.

Irwin-Zarecka, I. (1994). *Frames of remembrance: The dynamics of collective memory.* New Brunswick, NJ: Transaction Publishers.

Jackson-Opoku, S. (1997). *The river where blood is born.* New York: One World.

James, J. (1993). African philosophy, theory, and "living thinkers." In J. James & R. Farmer (Eds.), *Spirit, space and survival: African American women in (White) academe.* New York: Routledge.

Keating, A. (2008). "I'm a citizen of the universe": Gloria Anzaldúa's spiritual activism as catalyst for social change. *Feminist Studies,* 34(1/2): 53–69.

King, J. (Ed.). (2005). *Black education: A transformative research and action agenda for the new century.* Washington, DC: American Educational Research Association and Lawrence Erlbaum Publishers.

Kinloch, V. (2010). *Harlem on our minds: Place, race and the literacies of urban youth.* New York: Teachers College Press.

Krog, A. (2010). In the name of human rights: I say (how) you (should) speak (before I listen). In N. K. Denzin & M. Giardina (Eds.), *Qualitative inquiry and human rights.* Walnut Creek, CA: Left Coast Press.

Ladson-Billings, G. (2000). Racialized discourses and ethnic epistemologies. In N. K. Denzin & Y. S. Lincoln (Eds.), *The handbook of qualitative research.* Thousand Oaks, CA: Sage.

Ladson-Billings, G. & Donnor, J. (2005). The moral activist role of critical race theory. In N. K. Denzin & Y. S. Lincoln (Eds.), *The handbook of qualitative research.* Thousand Oaks, CA: Sage.

Lakoff, G. & Johnson, M. (1980). *Metaphors we live by.* Chicago: University of Chicago Press.

Lather, P. (2007). *Getting lost: Feminist efforts toward a double(d) science.* Albany, NY: State University of New York Press.

Latta, J. M. (1992). "Sacred songs as history." Interview with Bernice Johnson Reagon. Recorded August 4, 1992. Washington, DC: National Public Radio Archives, Wade in the Water Program.

Lemert, C. (Ed.). (2010). *Social theory: The multicultural and classic readings.* Boulder, CO: Westview Press.

Lorde, A. (1970). *Cables to rage.* London: Paul Breman.

Lorde, A. (1984). *Sister outsider: Essays and speeches by Audre Lorde.* Freedom, CA: The Crossing Press.

Lorde, A. (2009). There is no hierarchy of oppressions. In R. P. Byrd, J. B. Cole, & B. Guy-Sheftall (Eds.), *I am your sister: Collected and unpublished writings of Audre Lorde*. New York: Oxford University Press.

Madison, S. (2009). Dangerous ethnography. In N. Denzin & M. Giardina (Eds.), *Qualitative research and the conservative challenge*. Walnut Creek, CA: Left Coast Press.

Mama, A. (2007). Critical connections: Feminist studies in African contexts. In A. Cornwall, E. Harrison, & A. Whitehead (Eds.), *Feminisms in development: Contradictions, contestations and challenge*. London: Zeal Books.

Marshall, P. (1984). *Praisesong for the widow*. New York: Dutton.

Mazzei, L. A. (2007). *Inhabited silence in qualitative research: Putting poststructural theory to work*. New York: Peter Lang.

McElroy, C. J. (1997). *A long way from St. Louie: Travel memoirs*. Minneapolis: Coffee House Press.

Meyer, M. A. (2008). Indigenous and authentic: Hawaiian epistemology and the triangulation of meaning. In N. K. Denzin, Y. S. Lincoln, & L. Tuhiwai Smith (Eds.). *Handbook of critical and indigenous methodologies*. Thousand Oaks, CA: Sage.

Mohanty, C. T. (1991). Cartographies of struggle: Third world women and the politics of feminism. In C. T. Mohanty, A. Russo, and L. Torres (Eds.), *Third world women and the politics of feminism*. Bloomington: Indiana University Press.

Moraga, C. (1993). *The last generation*. Toronto, Canada: Canadian Scholars Press.

Moraga, C. & Anzaldúa, G. (1981). *This bridge called my back: Writings by radical women of color*. Watertown, MA: Persephone Press.

Morrison, T. (1970). *The bluest eye*. New York: Vintage Books.

Mountain Dreamer, O. (2005). *What we ache for: Creativity and the unfolding of the soul*. San Francisco: HarperCollins.

Moyers, B. D. & Pellett, G. (Producers). (1988). *Chinua Achebe*. New York: Public Affairs Television WNET.

Nnaemeka, O. (1998). *Sisterhood: Feminisms and power from Africa to the diaspora*. Trenton, NJ: Africa World Press.

Nwapa, F. (1966). *Efuru*. London: Cox and Wyman.

Nwapa, F. (1998). Women and creative writing in Africa. In O. Nnaemeka (Ed.), *Sisterhood: Feminisms and power from Africa to the diaspora*. Trenton, NJ: Africa World Press.

REFERENCES

Nzegwu, N. (2006). *Family matters: Feminist concepts in African philosophy of culture.* Albany, NY: State University of New York Press.

Obama, B. (2004). *Dreams from my father: A story of race and inheritance.* New York: Crown Publishers.

Ogola, M. (2004). *The river and the source.* Nairobi, Kenya: Focus Publications.

Ogundipe-Leslie, O. (1994). *Re-creating ourselves: African women and critical transformations.* Trenton, NJ: Africa World Press.

Okpalaoka, C. L. (2009). A cord of three strands is not easily broken: Endarkened feminist research and the linked experiences of Black women. Unpublished manuscript.

Okpalaoka, C. L. & Dillard, C. B. (2011). Our healing is next to the wound: Endarkened feminisms, spirituality, and wisdom for teaching and research. In E.J. Tisdell & A. Swartz (Eds.), *Adult education and the pursuit of wisdom.* New Directions in Adult and Continuing Education, no. 131. San Francisco: Jossey-Bass.

Omolade, B. (1994). *The rising song of African American women.* New York: Routledge.

Oyewumi, O. (1997). *The invention of women: Making an African sense of Western gender discourses.* Minneapolis: University of Minnesota Press.

Oyewumi, O. (2004). Conceptualizing gender: Eurocentric foundations of feminist concepts and the challenge of African epistemologies. In *CODESRIA, African gender scholarship: Concept, methodologies and paradigms.* Dakar, Senegal: CODESRIA.

Oyewumi, O. (2005). Visualizing the body: Western theories and African subjects. In O. Oyewumi (Ed.), *African gender studies: A reader.* New York: Palgrave Macmillan.

Palmer, P. (1993). *To know as we are known: Education as a spiritual journey.* San Francisco: Harper.

Palmer, P. (1998). *The courage to teach: Exploring the inner landscape of a teacher's life.* San Francisco: Jossey-Bass.

Paris, P. (1995). *The spirituality of African people: Towards a moral discourse.* Minneapolis, MN: Fortress Press.

Reason, P. (1993). Sacred experience and sacred sciences. *Journal of Management Inquiry,* 2: 10–27.

Reeves, D. (1999). *Testify.* On Bridges [CD]. New York: Blue Note Records.

Reid, V. (1999). Fashion may be momentary. In F. Mastalia & A. Pagano (Eds.), *Dreads.* New York: Artisan.

Rhee, J. (2008). Risking to be wounded again: Performing open eye/I. *Race, Ethnicity and Education,* 11, 1, 29–40.

Richards, D. (1980). *Let the circle be unbroken: The implications of African spirituality in the diaspora.* Lawrenceville, NJ: The Red Sea Press.

Rodriguez, J. & Fortier, T. (2007). *Cultural memory: Resistance, faith, and identity.* Austin: University of Texas Press.

Rogers, S. (2000). Embodying cultural memory in Paule Marshall's Praisesong for the widow. *African American Review,* 34, 1: 77–93.

Ryan, J. S. (2005). *Spirituality as ideology in Black women's film and literature.* Charlottesville: University of Virginia Press.

Ryrie, C. & Cavagnaro, D. (1999). *The healing energies of water.* Boston: Journey Editions.

Saavedra, C. M. & Nymark, E. D. (2008). Borderland-Mestizaje feminism: The new tradition. In N. K. Denzin, Y. S. Lincoln, & L. Tuhiwai Smith (Eds.), *Handbook of critical and indigenous methodologies.* Los Angeles: Sage.

Scheurich, J. & Young, M. (1997). Coloring epistemologies: Are our research epistemologies racially biased? *Educational Researcher,* 26: 4–16.

Shange, N. (1975). *For colored girls who considered suicide when the rainbow is enuf.* New York: Collier/Macmillan.

Singh, A., Skerrett, J. T., & Hogan, R. E. (Eds.) (1996). *Memory and cultural politics: New approaches to American ethnic literatures.* Lebanon, NH: Northeastern University Press.

Smith, B. (1983). *Home girls: A Black feminist anthology.* New York: Kitchen Table Women of Color Press.

Smith, L.T. (1999). *Decolonizing methodologies: Research and indigenous peoples.* London: Zed Books.

Sofola, Z. (1998). Feminism and African womanhood. In O. Nnaemeka (Ed.), *Sisterhood: Feminisms and power from Africa to the diaspora.* Trenton, NJ: Africa World Press.

Some, M. P. (1994). *Of water and the spirit: Ritual, magic, and initiation in the life of an African shaman.* New York: G. P. Putnam & Sons.

Soyinka, W. (1999). *The burden of memory, the muse of forgiveness.* New York: Oxford University Press.

Steady, F. C. (1981). The Black woman cross-culturally: An overview. In F. C. Steady (Ed.), *The Black woman cross-culturally*. Cambridge, MA: Schenkmann Publishing.

Steady, F. C. (1996). African feminism: A worldwide perspective. In R. Terbog-Penn & R. Benton (Eds.), *Women in Africa: A reader*. Washington, DC: Howard University Press.

Steady, F. C. (2004). An investigative framework for gender research in Africa in the new millennium. In CODESRIA, *African gender scholarship: Concepts, methodologies and paradigms*. Dakar, Senegal: CODESRIA.

Stilson, J. (Director). (2009). *Good hair* [Motion picture]. United States: Lionsgate.

Strong-Wilson, T. (2008). *Bringing memory forward: Storied remembrance in social justice education with teachers*. New York: Peter Lang.

Subedi, B. (2008). Contesting racialization: Asian immigrant teachers' critiques and claims of teacher authenticity. *Race, Ethnicity and Education*, 11, 1: 57–70.

Subreendeth, S. (2008). Deconstructing the politics of a differently colored transnational identity. *Race, Ethnicity and Education*, 11, 1: 41–56.

Sykes, W. & Stanton, L. (Executive Producers). (2009). *I'ma be me* [Comedy special]. United States: Home Box Office (HBO).

Taiwo, O. (2003). Reflections on the poverty of theory. In O. Oyewumi (Ed.), *African women and feminism: Reflecting on the politics of sisterhood*. Trenton, NJ: Africa World Press.

Taylor, J. B. (2009). *My stroke of insight: A brain scientist's personal journey*. Detroit, MI: Gale.

Trinh, T. M. (1989). *Woman native other: Writing postcoloniality and feminism*. Bloomington: Indiana University Press.

Tutu, D. (1999). *No future without forgiveness*. New York: Doubleday.

Tyson, C. A. (1998). A response to "Coloring epistemologies: Are our qualitative research epistemologies racially biased?" *Educational Researcher*, 27: 21–22.

Vanzant, I. (1993). *Acts of faith: Daily meditations for people of color*. New York: Fireside.

Wade-Gayles, G. (Ed.). (1995). *My soul is a witness: African-American women's spirituality*. Boston: Beacon Press.

Walker, A. (1983). *In search of our mothers' gardens: Womanist prose*. San Diego, CA: Harvest Books.

Walker, A. (1984). *Horses make the landscape more beautiful: Poems by Alice Walker*. San Diego, CA: Harcourt Brace Jovanovich.

Walker, A. (1988). *Living by the word: Selected writings 1973–1987*. Orlando, FL: Harcourt Brace Jovanovich.

Walker, A. (2006). *We are the ones we have been waiting for: Inner light in a time of darkness*. New York: The New Press.

Wallace, M. (1982). A Black feminist's search for sisterhood. In G. T. Hull, P. B. Scott, & B. Smith (Eds.), *All the women are White, all the Blacks are men, but some of us are brave: Black women's studies*. New York: The Feminist Press.

Weinstein, J. (Producer), & Washington, D. (Director). (2007). *The great debaters* [Motion picture]. United States: Harpo Films and Weinstein Company.

Wekker, G. (1997). One finger does not drink okra soup: Afro-Surinamese women and critical agency. In M. J. Alexander and C. T. Mohanty (Eds.), *Feminist genealogies, colonial legacies, democratic futures*. New York: Routledge.

West, C. (1994). *Race matters*. New York: Knopf/Doubleday.

Willis, B. (1998). *The Adinkra dictionary: A visual primer on the language of Adinkra*. Washington, DC: The Pyramid Complex.

Wilson, A. (2003). *The bead is constant*. Accra, Ghana: Ghana Universities Press.

Wolf, N. (1995). The racism of well meaning White people. In M. Golden & S. R. Shreve (Eds.), *Skin deep: Black women and White women write about race*. New York: Doubleday.

Wright, H. K. (2003). An endarkened feminist epistemology? Identity, difference and the politics of representation in educational research. *International Journal of Qualitative Research*, 16, 2: 197–214.

Wynter, S. (1990). *Do not call us Negros: How "multicultural" textbooks perpetuate racism*. San Francisco: Aspire.

Yoshino, K. (2006). *Covering: The hidden assault on our civil rights*. New York: Random House.